At Issue

Child Pornography

Other Books in the At Issue Series:

At Issue

Child Pornography

Amanda Hiber, Book Editor

GREENHAVEN PRESS
A part of Gale, Cengage Learning

GALE
CENGAGE Learning™

Detroit • New York • San Francisco • New Haven, Conn • Waterville, Maine • London

GALE
CENGAGE Learning

Christine Nasso, *Publisher*
Elizabeth Des Chenes, *Managing Editor*

© 2009 Greenhaven Press, a part of Gale, Cengage Learning.

Gale and Greenhaven Press are registered trademarks used herein under license.

For more information, contact:
Greenhaven Press
27500 Drake Rd.
Farmington Hills, MI 48331-3535
Or you can visit our Internet site at gale.cengage.com

Articles in Greenhaven Press anthologies are often edited for length to meet page requirements. In addition, original titles of these works are changed to clearly present the main thesis and to explicitly indicate the author's opinion. Every effort is made to ensure that Greenhaven Press accurately reflects the original intent of the authors. Every effort has been made to trace the owners of copyrighted material.

Cover photograph reproduced by permission of Illustration Works.

LIBRARY OF CONGRESS CATALOGING-IN-PUBLICATION DATA

Child pornography / Amanda Hiber, book editor.
   p. cm. -- (At issue)
   Includes bibliographical references and index.
   ISBN-13: 978-0-7377-4288-6 (hardcover)
   ISBN-13: 978-0-7377-4287-9 (pbk.)
   1. Child pornography. 2. Child pornography--Law and legislation. I. Hiber, Amanda.
   HQ471.C45 2009
   364.1'74--dc22
                                                        2008045078

Printed in the United States of America
1 2 3 4 5 6 7 13 12 11 10 09

Contents

Introduction

There is no debating that the growth of the Internet in the past 20 years has changed the ways child pornography is viewed, distributed, and produced. By most accounts, the Internet has made these crimes much easier to commit. Ernie Allen, president and CEO of the National Center for Missing and Exploited Children, has called the Internet "a child pornography superhighway." Regina B. Schofield captures the effect this has had on Americans' sense of security this way: "The reality that we once knew—a world in which the home was our safest haven—has given way to a new, virtual reality. The Internet now gives people from across the globe instant entrée into our homes and lives." For example, at a House Committee on Energy and Commerce hearing of the Oversight and Investigations Subcommittee in April 2006, witnesses testified that "sexual predators were preying on victims as young as 18 months by using instant messaging and Web cameras to meet, lure, and digitally stalk children and to share pornography," according to *New York Times* reporter Joshua Brockman.

Just as committing such crimes has become easier, catching and prosecuting those who commit them has become more difficult. Pornography's shift from print to cyberspace leaves little hard evidence to implicate offenders, or even to locate them. Writer Kevin G. Hall explains that consumers of child pornography only need to access illegal images from somewhere other than their own home to go a long way toward eluding law enforcement: "If you take a laptop to a free wireless hot spot that doesn't have any log-in requirements, the IP address is assigned to that establishment's wireless router. That makes it much harder for law enforcement to find out who was logged on to an illicit Web site or transferring illicit files at a given time from a given place," he says.

By accessing pornography at a public library or wireless café, consumers necessarily involve third parties in their crimes, even if that third party is unaware. Law enforcement officials and lawmakers have responded to this new set of circumstances with targeted laws and strategies. In 2000, President Bill Clinton signed into law the Children's Internet Protection Act (CIPA), which requires certain public libraries to install filters that prevent access to pornographic Web sites. This law was challenged in 2001 by the American Library Association, which argued that the law required libraries to block constitutionally protected material, but the Supreme Court upheld the law in 2003. This challenge was only one of many that have been, and continue to be, made to antipornography laws on the grounds that material deemed pornographic is protected by the First Amendment.

More recently, law enforcement officials have asked Internet service providers (ISPs) to help catch consumers and producers of child pornography by "root[ing] out people selling, trading, or displaying illegal pornographic images," explains Ron Scherer. "In fact, many of them already are cooperating, but some U.S. lawmakers, among others, want to go further: They want to require virtually all Internet mediums to provide tips the come across so cybercops can hunt down suspects," he says.

This potential mandate has drawn criticism from representatives of many ISPs, who complain that this requirement will cost them too much. As Hall explains, "Data retention also raises questions of who's liable when the security of stored data has been breached." Finally, as with other antipornography strategies, "Privacy advocates see data retention as a slippery slope," says Hall.

The difficult balance between the protection of children on one hand and protection of privacy on the other might have seemed achievable with the birth of *virtual* child pornography—that is, pornography that portrays children but does not, in reality, use children. Virtual child pornography is produced by making an adult appear to be a child, through makeup or digital manipulation of a photograph. Indeed, many make the argument that virtual pornography could result in declined child exploitation. According to U.S. Senator Orrin Hatch: "Critics of virtual child pornography regulation claim that viewing virtual pornography does not contribute to the abuse of real children. In fact, they argue that it diminishes such abuse by satisfying the appetites of pedophiles without the abuse or exploitation of children." But Hatch, like others, does not accept this argument: "Legalizing virtual child pornography, at a minimum, helps sustain a market for child pornography in general. Further, amongst the morass of virtual and actual images on the Internet and elsewhere, I have a hard time believing that the individuals who consume these materials will have the moral fortitude to restrict themselves only to virtual creations," he says.

Such concerns contributed to the creation and passage of the 1996 Child Pornography Prevention Act (CPPA), which criminalized images that appeared to be child pornography, even if they didn't, in fact, involve children. However, the Free Speech Coalition disputed this bill on constitutional grounds, and the Supreme Court ruled in favor of this argument, striking down CPPA in 2002. In response, Senator Hatch himself drafted a bill in 2003 that eventually became the PROTECT Act. This law, according to Wendy Kaminer, "includes a provision similar to the earlier ban on speech falsely 'convey[ing] the impression of child porn.'" The 11th Circuit Court of Appeals struck down the law, calling its language "vague and standardless." But the decision was appealed, and in May 2008, in *U.S. v. Williams*, the Supreme Court upheld the law, ruling that the bill does not violate First Amendment or other constitutional rights.

The *Williams* case encapsulates the paradox implicit in child pornography debates in the age of the Internet. At the same time that law enforcement is continually adapting its tactics to the changing landscape of child pornography, the subsequent debates largely revolve around an invariable tension: that between the protection of children and the protection of individual privacy. Furthermore, this reflects larger debates about the Constitution and what exactly is considered "free speech." As the Internet, which brings with it entirely new ways of conveying and receiving information, continues to grow, so does its impact on our lives and the impact of those issues of free speech and the right to privacy that it brings with it.

1

Law Enforcement Has Made Great Strides in Combating Child Pornography

Laura Bush

Laura Bush, first lady of the United States from 2001 to 2008, is a former teacher and librarian. As first lady, she worked on projects concerning education, literacy, women's health, and other issues.

The United States made a great stride toward helping missing and exploited children with the establishment of the National Center for Missing and Exploited Children in 1984. Today, 94 percent of children reported missing to the center are recovered. The AMBER Alert system is one component of the American law enforcement system that is facilitating this success rate. President George W. Bush also implemented new laws that increase the penalties for American citizens who prey on children abroad. The attorney general's Project Safe Childhood is expected to make a substantial impact in the fight against child pornography, as is the Innocent Images Initiative that connects law enforcement agencies in 17 countries to put a stop to global child pornography transactions. All countries must protect their own, and all, children from exploitation. These and other programs are part of the United States' vast effort toward ending child exploitation of all kinds.

Laura Bush, Remarks at the International Centre for Missing and Exploited Children Conference, Paris, France, *WhiteHouse.gov*, January 17, 2007. Reproduced by permission.

The United States made missing and exploited children a priority in 1981 when a young boy named Adam Walsh was kidnapped in a Florida department store. When Adam first disappeared, his parents had no network to call on to help to get their son back. Shortly after Adam's abduction, he was found murdered.

Adam's father, John Walsh, was determined that no parent should feel powerless to recover a missing child. His advocacy helped establish the National Center for Missing and Exploited Children, which has built an extraordinary network to keep families together.

Today, federal, state, and local law enforcement cooperate to pursue kidnappers across state lines. National registries alert parents about convicted sexual predators living in their neighborhoods. Across the United States, anyone can call a hotline to immediately report a missing child. In 1990, 62 percent of children reported missing to the center were recovered. Today, the number has climbed to 94 percent.

Pornographic images of children are . . . criminal acts of child abuse. The United States is working to end this abuse.

We saw the effectiveness of the National Center for Missing and Exploited Children in the aftermath of Hurricane Katrina. With help from the federal government, the American Red Cross, and many, many individual volunteers, the National Center worked day and night to reunite families separated by the storm. Of the more than 5,000 children initially reported missing, every single case of a missing child has been resolved, and this gives me the opportunity to thank Ernie Allen, the head of the National Center for Missing and Exploited Children in the United States.

In the United States, some of the most important work to recover missing children is done by the American people. Just last week in Missouri, a tip from an observant child led to the rescue of two kidnapped boys, one who had been missing for four days, and one who had been missing for four years. The rescue was aided by our country's AMBER [America's Missing: Broadcast Emergency Response] Alert system. Through AMBER Alerts, local law enforcement works with broadcast media and with transit authorities to make sure any American watching a TV or listening to a radio or passing a highway sign can help locate missing children. So far, AMBER Alerts have saved more than 300 young lives in the United States, and similar programs are now saving lives in countries across the globe, including France.

Government Action Is Necessary

All governments must do their part to end global threats to children, because the abuse of a child anywhere is an offense to civilized people everywhere. Every year, approximately one million children are trafficked for commercial sexual exploitation. Every country must educate its citizens, especially women and children, so they can avoid this degradation. Governments must also reduce the demand for child prostitution among their own citizens.

In recent years, President [George W.] Bush has signed into law increased penalties for U.S. citizens who travel abroad to engage in sexual exploitation of children. While the digital age presents new opportunities, it also poses new threats to young people. The Internet allows predators to make contact with unsuspecting children. It means the exploitation of children in one country can devastate families half a world away. It has turned child pornography into a global crisis.

Pornographic images of children are not exercises in free speech. They are criminal acts of child abuse. The United States is working to end this abuse through the government's Internet Crimes Against Children task forces. With the help of task force members, federal prosecution of child pornography and abuse has increased from 350 cases in 1998 to more than 1,400 cases in 2005.

We expect even more advances in this fight against child pornography through our government's new Project Safe Childhood program. Announced by Attorney General Alberto Gonzalez in February 2006, Project Safe Childhood has launched a coordinated national response to the growing threat of online exploitation. Federal, state and local law enforcement cooperate to secure the strictest possible penalties against sexual predators. Project Safe Childhood is also partnering with the National Center for Missing and Exploited Children and the Ad Council to start a public awareness campaign that will teach parents and children how to avoid predators online.

Countries Must Cooperate with Each Other

Through our national and international Innocent Images Initiative, the American government works with law enforcement in 17 nations, as well as Europol, to end the nearly nine million documented global transactions of child pornography.

The abuses of children on the Internet respect no national boundaries. And we've seen that when governments cooperate with other nations, they keep children in their own countries safe.

A society shows its character in the way it treats its most vulnerable citizens.

In 2003, this international cooperation saved the life of a six-year-old American girl. In Denmark, a law enforcement officer discovered images online of this little girl being abused, and he reported them to Interpol. Within days, the images were recognized by the Toronto police service, which worked with American officials to decipher clues about the little girl's identity. The FBI examined pictures taken of the girl in her Scout uniform, traced the troop number in the photos, and followed the images to North Carolina. There they found the little girl, and the relative who had abused her, and he is now serving a 100-year sentence.

In the more than 175,000 images this man had on his computer, law enforcement found evidence that led to the arrest of child abusers in South Carolina, Texas, and the United Kingdom. Because one person in Denmark tipped off Interpol, four children in the United States were saved.

A society shows its character in the way it treats its most vulnerable citizens. Each of us can help protect children in our societies, and every country must help protect children in our global society.

2

Law Enforcement Needs to Do More to Stop Child Pornography

Ernie Allen

Ernie Allen is the president and chief executive officer of the National Center for Missing and Exploited Children. Previously, he served as the director of public health and safety for the city of Louisville, Kentucky.

Children are the most victimized group in America, particularly by sex offenders, a fact that the majority of Americans would rather not acknowledge. While the federal government is addressing this problem more actively than ever before, it is still not doing enough. This is especially true in the realm of Internet predators and child pornography. The National Center for Missing and Exploited Children has established several mechanisms to eradicate child pornography, such as the Financial Coalition Against Child Pornography, but the federal government must do more to prosecute as well as deter child predators and pornographers from exploiting America's most vulnerable population.

On Monday [December 4, 2006] Attorney General [Alberto] Gonzales sent a loud, clear message that even in this time of national concern about terrorism and so many other problems, the protection of children is a top priority. He told us that America's children are "under siege every day," and that that we have to do more to target those predators who "hide in the shadows of the Internet."

Ernie Allen, Closing speech at Project Safe Childhood Conference, Washington, D.C., *National Center for Missing & Exploited Children*, December 6, 2006. Reproduced by permission.

In what I believe is a clear profile in courage, General Gonzales has taken this message across the country, speaking in tough, vivid, often graphic terms, describing the atrocities being committed against children so that people really understand. His goal is to spur the nation to act. . . .

As the attorney general told us Monday, we are not doing enough.

These are issues and problems that good people do not want to think about and regarding which there is an overwhelming sense of denial. For example, I submit that most Americans still do not understand a fundamental fact: that kids are the single most victimized segment of our population. They are the victims of violent and personal crime at a rate twice as great as the rest of the population. They are the primary victims of the nation's sex offenders. And the challenge is growing.

Here is what we know:

Leading scholars and researchers tell us that on the most conservative basis, 1 in 5 girls and 1 in 10 boys will be sexually victimized in some way before they reach adulthood, and just 1 in 3 will tell anybody about it.

As of December 1, 2006, there are 593,000 convicted, registered sex offenders in the U.S. At least 100,000 of them are noncompliant with legal requirements, many of them actually missing.

According to Justice Department data, two-thirds of the victims of reported sexual assault are kids. One out of every three victims is under age 12.

A study by the National Center for Victims of Crime estimated that 61% of rape victims are less than 18, 29% less than 11.

Better but Still Not Enough

It is daunting but it is not hopeless. We are making progress. The federal government is doing more on these issues today than at any time in the nation's history. We have an attorney general who is committed and cares. With the enactment of the PROTECT [Prosecutorial Remedies and Other Tools to End the Exploitation of Children Today] Act in 2003 and the Adam Walsh Act in 2006, there is new law, new prosecutorial tools and significant new federal penalties. We have more investigative resources than ever before: 47 Internet Crimes Against Children task forces, an expanding Innocent Images National Initiative at the FBI, a CyberCrimes Center at ICE [Immigration and Customs Enforcement], dedicated investigators at the U.S. Postal Inspection Service, a new effort headed by the U.S. Marshals Service and mandated by the Adam Walsh Act to track down America's noncompliant sex offenders, new specialized units within state and local law enforcement across the country, and much more. There are many exciting, effective new programs to educate parents and kids and to prevent child victimization via the Internet, and there is a greater commitment to collaboration and cooperation than ever before.

Yet, as the attorney general told us Monday, we are not doing enough. There are more offenders than any of us thought possible. There is a lack of consistency and uniformity of law among the states. There is a lack of awareness about the nature and severity of this problem among policy makers and the general public.

How can we impact problems which are so large and complex? Let me briefly focus my comments on two key areas:

1. Online Enticement of Children—According to our recent study, one in seven youth aged 10 to 17 who are regular Internet users are sexually solicited online. That translates to millions of kids, and it suggests that there are thousands of offenders whom we have not yet identified and brought to justice.

Do Whatever It Takes

The attorney general told us on Monday that we must use whatever law is most effective, whatever law generates the largest number of convictions and the longest sentences.

Under federal law, online enticement is a felony punishable by a minimum prison term of 10 years and a maximum of life imprisonment. However, while all 50 states consider the online enticement of a child for sexual activity a crime, the penalties vary widely from state to state and may range from a simple fine to life in prison.

In 34 states, adults who entice children for sex via the Internet may spend less than a year in jail.

Fifteen states permit misdemeanor penalties in some cases, particularly if the victim is 14, 15, 16, or 17 years old. This is a huge problem because these laws fail to protect those who are the most likely to be solicited online: teenagers.

Nineteen states classify online enticement as a felony, but grant judges statutory discretion to sentence offenders to less than a year. In fifteen states, judges have statutory discretion to sentence offenders to simply pay a fine in lieu of serving time in prison.

We believe that these disparities create loopholes for criminals. They allow sexual predators to find states with the most lenient laws and to carry out their illicit activities from those locations. Further, inconsistent laws have little deterrent effect, because they send mixed messages.

To better protect children from online predators, we urge states to use the federal law as the model and make the sexual enticement of children a felony in all cases—even when the victims are older teens—and follow federal sentencing guidelines.

We also recommend that laws stipulate that offenders must be prosecuted, even in cases involving law enforcement enticement stings. In too many instances we still hear, "it wasn't really a child." The offender didn't know that. These law enforcement officers are often the buffer between the offenders and real children.

We need a unified front against online predators. To be effective, state online enticement laws must be tough and consistent and penalties must include prison time that recognizes the severity of the crime.

Child Pornography Has Exploded

2. Child Pornography—In 1982 the Supreme Court of the United States said that child pornography is not protected speech, it is child abuse. Law enforcement responded and child pornography disappeared from the mail and the shelves of adult bookstores. Ten years ago, we felt that the battle was nearly won. Yet, with the advent of the Internet, this problem has exploded. We have been stunned with the sheer number of people who are accessing and distributing this insidious content. It far exceeds what we thought possible.

A 2001 survey conducted by ECPAT [End Child Prostitution, Child Pornography and Trafficking of Children for Sexual Purposes] International and the *Bangkok Post* estimated that there were 100,000 child pornography Web sites.

In 2003, the National Criminal Intelligence Service in the United Kingdom estimated that child pornography web sites had doubled worldwide.

Children have become a commodity.

Economic research organizations tell us that today commercial child pornography is a multibillion dollar industry.

In one case that I cite frequently, at the time of their arrest, two husband and wife child pornography entrepreneurs had 70,000 customers, paying $30 per month and using their credit cards to access graphic images of young children being sexually assaulted. Senator Richard Shelby of Alabama, the chairman of the Senate Banking Committee, said it best:

> *If people were purchasing heroin or cocaine and using their credit cards, we would be outraged and would do something about it. This is worse.*

It is clear that the sexual exploitation of children is no longer the exclusive province of fixated pedophiles, trading images with each other, it is now big business, a profit center for organized crime, extremist groups, and various entrepreneurs. Children have become a commodity.

In a recent article, the Russian publication *Pravda* cited five reasons for this phenomenon:

1. Children are plentiful and easily accessed;
2. Child pornography is easy and inexpensive to produce;
3. There is a huge consumer market for it;
4. It is enormously profitable; and
5. There is virtually no risk, far less than traditional commodities like drugs, guns, and tobacco.

Greater Understanding Needed

Our challenge is to increase the risk and eliminate the profitability.

Yet, to do that, it is our task to make sure that policy makers and the public understand the problem. One official said to me, "Isn't child pornography really just adult pornography, 20-year-olds in pigtails made to look like they are 15?" Well, not exactly. We know that younger and younger children are being used and victimized, and that images are becoming more graphic and more violent. Of the offenders identified to date, 39% had images of children younger than six years old, and 19% had images of children younger than 3.

We have set a goal: to eradicate commercial child pornography by 2008. We have created a Financial Coalition Against Child Pornography, including MasterCard, Visa, American Express, Bank of America, Citibank, Microsoft, AOL, Yahoo, Google and many others—27 companies working together to follow the money, stop the payments, shut down the sites, block the images, and eliminate this insidious problem.

In most of the world, child pornography is not even a crime. In 95 of the 186 member nations of Interpol, there are no laws at all on this subject. Recently, I met with a group of Russian legislators to urge them to enact tough legislation in this area. A Russian senator said to me, "We will help, but you need to do something about the demand. The people who are buying this stuff are Americans."

She is right, and we need to do something about it. We need to arrest and prosecute those who are consuming it. We need to identify the children being used in its production and get them help. And we need to use every possible tool to keep this content from ever reaching the consumer.

This is a challenge we can and must accept, and this is a cause that we can win.

We are trying to do that. For example, we are working with Internet service providers to block access to identified illegal content, again only after law enforcement has made its decision to investigate or not investigate.

Use Every Tool

Arrest and prosecution are always the first priority, but as in the war against drugs, it is not going to be possible to prosecute everybody. In those cases, we need to use every tool imaginable.

On Monday, the attorney general laid out his vision:

1. Get the pedophiles and sexual predators off the streets;

2. Increase the penalties and keep them behind bars; and

3. Engage in what he called "old-fashioned communication." He said, "We must speak and speak again and speak more loudly."

This is a challenge we can and must accept, and this is a cause that we can win. So, in conclusion, let me challenge you to do more.

When the National Center for Missing and Exploited Children . . . was officially opened on June 13, 1984, in a ceremony at the White House hosted by the president of the United States, Ronald Reagan. President Reagan officially opened the center with an old, corny poem by Helen Kromer, but I submit that it is as relevant and applicable today as it was 22 years ago.

One man awake can awaken another
The second can awaken his next
door brother
The three awake can rouse the
town
Turning the whole place upside
down
And the many awake make such a
fuss
They finally awaken the rest of
us. . . .

Help us wake up America.

3

Possession of Child Pornography Is Punished Too Harshly

Alexander Cockburn

Alexander Cockburn has written the "Beat the Devil" column for The Nation *since 1984. The author of many books, he is also the co-founder and co-editor of the political Web site and newsletter* CounterPunch.

There is an inverse relation between how a society treats its children and the extent to which it goes after child pornographers. For example, in 2003 the George W. Bush administration proposed millions of cuts in social services for children. At the same time, Paul Reubens, a.k.a. Pee-Wee Herman, was being charged with pornography possession for his collection of vintage erotica. But because Reubens, like all collectors, bought his materials in bulk, he could not possibly have known the full content of all that he bought. Still, the charges brought against him could have sent him to jail for a year. Likewise, singer Pete Townshend was recently arrested after using a credit card to obtain images from child pornography Web sites. In England, where he resides, it is illegal to send or receive any images of children, whether they are real or computer-generated. Such laws amount to a society that prosecutes its citizens for "thought crimes." There are, in fact, real predators in the world who pose real threats to children. These are the people who should be targeted, not those who merely engage in dreams or fantasies without acting on them.

The worse the state treats kids, the more the state's prosecutors chase after inoffensive "perverts" in the private sector who have committed the so-called crime of getting sexual kicks out of images downloaded into their computers or bought as part of an archive of archaic soft-core porn.

Before we get to [actor] Paul Reubens, a.k.a. Pee-Wee Herman, pause to consider the [George W. Bush] Administration's proposed cuts in social services affecting youth, as passed by the Senate in January [2003]:

- $60.9 million cut from childcare, meaning access cut for 38,000 kids;

- $29 million cut from after-school programs;

- $13 million cut from programs that help abused and neglected children;

- $3 million cut from children's mental health funding;

- $42 million cut from substance-abuse treatment programs.

All this and more from a President who had the effrontery in his State of the Union address to proclaim the ringing lie, "We will not pass along our problems" to future generations, even as the future generations are scheduled to pick up the tab for his proposed disbursements to the very rich.

Meanwhile, out in California a prosecutor is trying once more to destroy Pee-Wee, who took a hit back in 1991 for the awful crime of masturbating in a Sarasota film theater during a showing of *Nancy Nurse*. Reubens pleaded no contest and slowly hauled himself out of the ditch, but last year the shadows gathered round him once more. His travails were recently described by Richard Goldstein in a brilliant piece in the *Village Voice*.

A teenager complained to the LAPD [Los Angeles Police Department] about Reubens and a friend, the actor Jeffrey Jones. Though the complaint was dismissed, cops took the occasion to search the homes of both men. Jones is charged with taking pornographic pictures of a juvenile, a felony. Reubens faces a lesser charge: possession. Both have pleaded not guilty.

Dubious Charges

But what exactly does Reubens "possess"? He collects vintage erotica, mostly gay, with copies of those old physique mags that slaked covert gay fantasies the same way Naked Women of Borneo in *National Geographic* helped out straight kids in the same era. The cops took away 30,000 items for leisurely perusal, leaving behind a further 70,000. The DA [District Attorney] concluded there was no case, and it looked as though Pee-Wee was in the clear.

Reubens may get cooked for images he didn't even know he had.

Enter a zealous Protector of Youth in the form of the city attorney, Rocky Delgadillo. One day before the one-year statute of limitations expired, Delgadillo issued a warrant for Reubens's arrest. If Reubens gets convicted he could go to prison for a year. Goldstein writes that the cops told him Reubens had 6,500 hours of videotape, including transfers of vintage 8-millimeter gay films, with some minutes of teenage boys masturbating or having oral sex. Remember, in 1982 the Supreme Court declared child pornography unprotected by the First Amendment, with "porn" encompassing even clothed images of children if they are construed as arousing. "Child" means anyone under 18.

Collectors buy archives in bulk. An archive comes up and you grab it quick. Goldstein cites a California dealer of vintage magazines, who has sold to Reubens, as saying "there's no way" he could have known the content of each page in the publications he bought. In other words, Reubens may get cooked for images he didn't even know he had. But what if he actually did know what he had? So what?

"Thought Crimes"

The state these days nails people for what they have in their computers. Poor Pete Townshend draws a well-publicized escort of no less than twelve police officers to drag him off when he's arrested and absurdly accused of "incitement to distribute" (also a crime here) because the silly ass used a credit card to download images from pedophile sites, which are monitored by the FBI in a vast operation involving multilayered schemes of entrapment.

In England it's now a criminal act to look at, receive or send any pictures or electronic images of children that the police or other authorities construe as sex related. These photos can be computer-generated, with no relation to any physical being. Scan a hot little Cupid from Bouguereau, tweak it around in Photoshop, and if the cops find it on your laptop you're dead meat.

Don't confuse dreams with deeds.

We're in the twilit world of the "thought crime." Have a photo of a kid in a bath on your hard drive, and the prosecutor says you were looking at it with lust in your heart, and that is tantamount to sexually molesting an actual kid in an actual bath. The possibilities for entrapment are rich indeed. The FBI could send pedophilic images to a target, then rush around, seize his laptop and announce that porn has been found on the hard drive. Once you're defined as a dirty brute in a raincoat, it's hard to fight back. Look at what's happening to [former United Nations weapons inspector] Scott Ritter, with the Feds now shopping for a suitable jurisdiction in which to nail him again, even though his case was settled and sealed at the state level, before some kind soul in favor of bombing kids in Baghdad leaked the file to the press.

Dreams vs. Deeds

In an admirable article in the *London Daily Telegraph* apropos the Townshend case, Barbara Amiel recently wrote thus:

> Behind our own attitudes lurks a recurring insistence that violent images create violent social behaviour. . . . Since we can't outlaw urges, including urges of paedophilia, we throw our resources into preventing any way in which urges can be gratified. But, if gratification involves nothing else than the viewing of pictures or textual descriptions of the act, making that a criminal offence strikes one as completely insane. Shouldn't we start by decriminalising every human act that does not go beyond reading, viewing or listening to representations of acts that if engaged in might be unlawful? Then we could punish with various degrees of severity any deviant acts that cause actual harm.

Sure, there are predators out there, seeking to do young people harm. But don't confuse dreams with deeds, any more than we should confuse George Bush's pledge to future generations that "we will not pass along our problems" with the pain his budgets and his war plans inflict on so many young lives.

4

Possession of Child Pornography Is Punished Too Lightly in Canada

Julian Sher

Julian Sher is an award-winning documentary producer, true-crime writer, speaker, and journalist. He is the author of numerous investigative books, the most recent of which is One Child at a Time: The Global Fight to Rescue Children from Online Predators.

In 2006, law enforcement in several countries cooperated to bust a global child pornography ring called Kiddypics, resulting in more than 80 arrests. Yet two years after the arrests, it was revealed that while other countries had sentenced offenders to decades in prison, Canadian sentences amounted to a matter of days. This outcome is not atypical; there are numerous examples of child pornographers receiving sentences that are a mere fraction of what they would receive in other countries. Even among those who commit child sexual abuse, there is a striking discrepancy between Canadian sentences and those issued elsewhere. One former prosecutor says that in Canada, someone convicted of robbing a bank will spend more time in prison than someone convicted of abusing a child.

In the murky underworld of Internet chat rooms where collaborators trade in graphic images of child abuse, he was

Julian Sher, "Facing Light Punishment," *Maclean's*, April 7, 2008, pp. 24–25. Copyright © 2008 by *Maclean's Magazine*. Reproduced by permission of the author.

known as "Lord Vader." Even by the depraved standards of Internet child porn, the "Kiddypics and Kiddyvids" club where he hung out was egregious. Members used sophisticated encryption to view sexually exploitative material—including live streaming video of men abusing their own infant children. In one post monitored by police who infiltrated the group, Lord Vader boasted that he had "lots of fun" watching young children at a local shopping mall. "Perv?" joked another Kiddypics member. "Thanks for the compliment," Vader replied.

It was no joking matter back in March 2006 when—thanks to intensive undercover work by Canadian investigators who have gained a reputation worldwide for their cyber-skills—authorities here as well as in the U.S., Australia and Europe announced they had broken up the Kiddypics ring, which was engaged in what the U.S. attorney general at the time called "the worst imaginable forms of child pornography." Eventually, more than 80 people were arrested around the world and over 30 children rescued in the landmark global police operation. Codenamed Project Wickerman, it remains one the biggest global busts of its kind.

But two years after the Wickerman arrests, a *Maclean's* survey of more than two dozen completed court cases reveals that while offenders in other countries face decades behind bars, their Canadian partners in crime can count their punishment in days.

Lord Vader turned out to be Kristan Hayes Ahola, now 30, who studied welding at a community college in Prince George, B.C. He pleaded guilty in British Columbia's provincial court to one count of "simple possession" of hundreds of abuse images; the Crown and defence made a joint submission for the sentence handed down in January [2008]. His punishment? Fourteen days—to be served on weekends. Ahola will also be on probation for three years and remain on Canada's Sex Offender Registry for 10 years.

Short Sentences for Possession

Those convicted of hands-on sexual assault of children generally get harsher punishments, but up until recently, many found guilty of so-called "simple possession" of child abuse images got no jail time at all. Fourteen days is the new minimum mandatory for the crime since 2006. "It's very frustrating," says Sgt. Paul Krawczyk, who until recently was a detective with Toronto's elite sex crimes unit. He spent months tracking down Lord Vader and other suspects in the Kiddypics chat room. "Canada is where the Wickerman case started," he says, "and where most of the work was done, and yet here is where we're getting the lowest sentences."

Like Lord Vader, two other Canadians found guilty of possession of child abuse images got only 14 days—even though one of them had one of the largest collections police had seen. "These are not 'just pictures,'" says Edmonton police Det. Randy Wickins, who worked closely with Krawczyk to launch the international bust. "I wish people could understand the horror of what these children go through." Three other Canadian men charged with distributing in addition to possessing the illicit images received 18-month terms.

The disparity between sentences in Canada and abroad is alarming.

Contrast that with the U.S., where nine people convicted of similar charges of possession and distribution in the Project Wickerman sweep are serving prison terms ranging from five to 20 years. "The children raped in these images are real, and we take these offences seriously," says Drew Oosterbaan, chief of the child exploitation and obscenity section at the Department of Justice in Washington. "You download child pornography, you should expect to do serious time." In Britain, three men found guilty received "indeterminate sentences"—meaning they stay behind bars indefinitely, until they prove they are no longer a danger to society.

Canadian Sentences Comparatively Light

Meanwhile, a Canadian ringleader of the group, an Edmonton man who was one of the chat room administrators, got off lightly. It was his arrest by Canadian investigators in early 2006 that led to the unravelling of the worldwide network. When police burst through his door, Carl Treleaven had 90 people standing by online, waiting to download some of the 20 gigabytes of child exploitation material he had stored on his computer. Treleaven, now 51, was released last September into a special residential treatment program for sex offenders, after serving only 18 months of a 3½-year sentence.

Treleaven's criminal record included two previous convictions for indecent assault and gross indecency. Indeed, there is some indication that the distinction between so-called "just pictures" offenders and physical, hands-on abusers may not be as great as imagined. A study by American psychologists with the Bureau of Prisons who worked with over 100 men convicted only of possessing pictures found that 85 per cent of them later confessed, while under treatment, to having committed some kind of sexual offence against a child.

Yet, even when it comes to abusers who directly inflict suffering on children, the disparity between sentences in Canada and abroad is alarming. The sole Canadian charged with sexual assault during the Kiddypics investigation was a St. Thomas, Ont., man whose name cannot be revealed, in order to protect the identity of his victim, his own infant daughter. The judge decried his actions as a "gross case" and "sickening"—and sentenced the abuser to four years. (The maximum penalty under Canadian law for sexual offences against children is 10 years, except for incest, which can carry a 14-year term.)

But when Canadian investigators Krawczyk and Wickins went down to the United States to testify against two other men in the club who also filmed their rape of their own children, the results were startlingly different: a court in Idaho sent one offender away for life and the other in Michigan for 120 years. Even in the traditionally liberal Netherlands, a Kiddypics member was sent to prison for 10 years for abusing two children.

Problem Not Being Addressed

"The sad truth is that in Canada, you are likely to spend more time behind bars if you rob a bank of a few thousand dollars than if you abuse a child," says David Butt, a former Ontario prosecutor and now world general secretary of ECPAT [End Child Prostitution, Child Pornography and Trafficking of Children for Sexual Purposes], an international organization that fights child exploitation and trafficking. "The bank's losses are fully insured. The child is usually scarred for life. What does that say about our justice system?"

Once he was exposed as a Kiddypics member, Kristan Ahola faced angry demonstrations outside his home in Prince George and was forced to leave the city, according to court documents. He "expressed shame and remorse" and began attending weekly psychological counselling sessions, the judge said. But if Ahola finds good help and sticks to it, he's the exception. "We're not getting enough treatment to the people who need it," says Dr. John Bradford, who treats high-risk offenders at the Sexual Behaviours Clinic at the Royal Ottawa Hospital. "Why are we not doing more about it? Because people don't want to face up to it as a public health problem."

An Ineffective System

The Justice department says it's monitoring 2005 Criminal Code amendments that boosted penalties for child porn cases as well as more recent sentencing reforms aimed at preventing repeat offenders. But the NDP [New Democratic Party] complains the system is not working. "We need to give police and prosecutors the proper resources so they can identify the severe cases," says justice critic Joe Comartin. As for those who actually opt for treatment, he says, sentences must be long enough for them to get into available programs.

Back in Edmonton, Det. Randy Wickins doesn't have time to worry about what happens to child predators after he arrests them. The team he works with at the RCMP's [Royal Canadian Mounted Police] integrated child exploitation unit already has 55 new criminal files on their desks and another 45 cases that they have not had time to even look at. "The reason we're doing this is not for the sentences," he says grimly. "The reason we're doing this is to rescue children."

5

The PROTECT Act Violates First Amendment Rights

Frederick Lane

Frederick Lane is a writer, speaker, and journalist who deals with the legal and cultural implications of new technology. He is the author of several books, including the most recent, The Court and the Cross: The Religious Right's Crusade to Reshape the Supreme Court.

The Supreme Court's recent ruling in United States v. Williams, *that the PROTECT Act is constitutional, is yet another decision that encroaches on the First Amendment under the guise of protecting children. Under U.S. law, child pornography is the only form of speech that is not protected by the First Amendment. While it was once relatively simple to discern legal from illegal images, the age of computers, the Internet, and digital cameras has seriously complicated the issue by blurring the line between artificial and real images. The PROTECT Act, passed by Congress as a replacement for the Child Pornography Prevention Act, which was ruled unconstitutional by the high court, prohibits presenting material in a way that leads someone to believe that it contains child pornography. In their dissent in the* United States v. Williams *case, Justices David Souter and Ruth Bader Ginsburg argued that the act violates the constitution because it would allow someone to be prosecuted for selling an image that a buyer believes to be illegal, even if it is not. While child pornography is indeed a serious crime, Justice Souter is right in his assertion that this law seriously threatens the First Amendment by enabling the prosecution of someone based on what he or she thinks.*

Roughly a month ago [May 19, 2008], the United States Supreme Court handed down a decision in *United States v. Williams* that upheld the consitutionality of the Prosecutorial Remedies and Other Tools to End the Exploitation of Children Today Act of 2003 (The PROTECT Act). The 7-2 decision is the latest in a disturbing line of Congressional actions and Supreme Court decisions that cloak encroachments on the First Amendment in the pious garb of protecting children.

A little background is useful in understanding the implications of the Williams decision. It is fair to say that the United States is unparalleled among the nations of the world in its tolerance of speech. From the instant it is uttered, virtually all speech is presumed to be protected by the First Amendment. That presumption can be overcome, but only if a prosecutor or plaintiff can prove that the speech falls into one the recognized exceptions to the First Amendment: libel or slander, for instance, or obscenity.

There is only one category of speech that does not enjoy the presumption of First Amendment protection: child pornography, which has traditionally been defined as sexually explicit visual depictions of individuals under the age of 18. If a prosecutor can prove that the subject of a sexually explicit photograph, for instance, is under the age of 18 then, regardless of how artistic or socially significant the photo may be, it is still "obscene" and not protected by the First Amendment.

Criminalizing Possession

In response to a surge in the production and distribution of child pornography in the late 1970s and early 1980s, the federal and state governments passed laws making it a crime to possess child pornography. Although the Supreme Court has held that mere possession of obscenity is protected by the First Amendment, it agreed that possession of child pornography could be barred.

New technologies have ... blurred the previously bright line between legal and illegal images.

"The prevention of sexual exploitation and abuse of children," Justice Byron White wrote, "constitutes a government objective of surpassing importance." Among other things, he noted, the New York legislature found that child pornography serves as a "permanent record" of abuse, a harm that is perpetuated by continued circulation of the images. The legislature also declared (and the Court agreed) that penalizing consumers would lessen demand for child pornography and help to fight its production. Regardless of one's position on the political spectrum, there is virtually no disagreement that a ban on both the production and possession of actual child pornography is a good social policy.

The Court's ratification of a flat ban on child pornography had a relatively minimal impact on the First Amendment. Admittedly, the ruling did cause serious problems for some photographers, ranging from parents taking innocuous photos of their children to fine art photographers whose works included nude photos of children (among the more well-known examples are David Hamilton, Jock Sturges, and Sally Mann). But on the whole, it was relatively easy to draw a bright line between legal and illegal images, and law enforcement made substantial progress in fighting child pornography.

Computer Age Presents New Challenges

Most of those gains, however, have been wiped out by computers, the Internet, and digital cameras, all of which have made the production and distribution of child pornography vastly easier and far more difficult to combat. These new technologies have also blurred the previously bright line between legal and illegal images: many websites feature very young-looking but still adult models; some individuals use software to blend two or more legal images into composite child pornography; and others use animation software to create completely artificial (but increasingly realistic) child pornography images.

In 1996, Congress adopted the Child Pornography Prevention Act as part of an omnibus appropriations bill. Among other things, the CPPA made it a crime to possess or distribute digital representations of minors engaged in sexual activity, even if the persons in the image were not actual minors. In *Ashcroft v. Free Speech Coalition* (2002), however, the Supreme Court ruled (by a 6-1-2 vote) that the CPPA was unconstitutional because it criminalized speech legitimately protected by the First Amendment.

"The CPPA," Justice [Anthony] Kennedy wrote, "prohibits speech despite its serious literary, artistic, political, or scientific value. The statute proscribes the visual depiction of an idea—that of teenagers engaging in sexual activity—that is a fact of modern society and has been a theme in art and literature throughout the ages."

The Court's decision was widely criticized by conservatives, and in particular, by the evangelical wing of the Republican Party, which has been at the forefront of Congressional efforts to restrict sexual materials online. It is no accident that in a 2008 speech on judicial activism, Senator John McCain alluded to the Free Speech Coalition decision as an example of activist judges.

Congress Passes a New Law

In response to the Free Speech Coalition decision, Congress passed the PROTECT Act, which dropped the outright ban on "virtual" child pornography. Instead, the law makes it illegal to advertise or present any material in such a way as to lead someone to believe that the material contains "an obscene visual depiction of a minor engaging in sexually explicit conduct," or "a visual depiction of an actual minor engaging in sexually explicit conduct."

"Both the State and Federal Governments have sought to suppress it for many years," Justice Antonin Scalia wrote, "only to find it proliferating through the new medium of the Internet. This Court held unconstitutional Congress's previous attempt to meet this new threat, and Congress responded with a carefully crafted attempt to eliminate the First Amendment problems we identified. As far as the provision at issue in this case is concerned, that effort was successful."

The dissent in Williams was written by the Supreme Court justice the Religious Right most despises, David Souter. Along with Justice Ruth Bader Ginsburg, Souter argued that the PROTECT Act is constitutionally flawed because an individual could be prosecuted for advertising or selling an image that is not itself illegal (a sexually explicit photograph, for instance, that does not depict actual children), but which the buyer or seller simply believes is illegal.

Even the Religious Right should be wary of a law that for the first time makes it possible to prosecute someone for what they merely think.

"We should hold that a transaction in what turns out to be fake pornography is better understood," Justice Souter said, "not as an incomplete attempt to commit a crime, but as a completed series of intended acts that simply do not add up to a crime, owing to the privileged character of the material the parties were in fact about to deal in."

A Threat to the First Amendment

While recognizing the gravity of the problem being addressed by Congress, Souter suggested that the harm to the First Amendment is much more significant. Traditionally, he said, limitations on speech are grounded on "realistic, factual assessments of harm." Instead, the PROTECT Act bases its criminal prosecutions on "nothing more than a speaker's statement about the material itself, a statement that may disclose no more than his own belief about the subjects represented or his desire to foster belief in another."

"First Amendment freedoms," Justice Souter quoted from the Free Speech Coalition case, "are most in danger when the government seeks to control thought or to justify its laws for that impermissible end. The right to think is the beginning of freedom, and speech must be protected from the government because speech is the beginning of thought."

It is worth reiterating time and again that child pornography is a serious crime and a growing problem for law enforcement, and that all available resources should be devoted to preventing its production and prosecuting its distribution. But even the Religious Right should be wary of a law that for the first time makes it possible to prosecute someone for what they merely think.

6

The PROTECT Act Does Not Violate First Amendment Rights

Mario Diaz

Mario Diaz, an attorney, is the policy director for legal issues at Concerned Women for America.

The 2008 United States v. Williams *Supreme Court case began with Michael Williams being charged with the possession, promotion, and distribution of child pornography. He appealed his conviction, calling the law under which he was charged, unconstitutional. He argued that the law was so vague that it could be applied to content that was not, in actuality, child pornography. Appropriately, the high court justices did not buy this challenge, nor did they accept the larger claim that the law restricts free speech. When the justices questioned Williams's attorney, it was made clear how tenuous his argument really was. It was indeed so reliant on theory and hypothetical situations, that when the justices pressed the attorney on specifics, he was at a loss. Ultimately, the high court rightly ruled that the law in question does not threaten free speech. After all, the government's obligation is to protect all children, not the occasional hypothetical person who feels his or her First Amendment rights are under attack.*

It ended [in October 2007] with an awkward silence and a puzzled look on the Justices' faces. Apparently, Mr. Richard Diaz (no relation to this author), counsel for the Respondent

Mario Diaz, "Protect Children, Not Charlatans," *Concerned Women for America*, May 20, 2008. Reproduced by permission.

in *U.S. v Williams*, had no other argument to make. Everyone in the room was stunned, and after a couple of seconds, though it seemed like an eternity, he thanked the Justices and sat down.

It was the unhappy ending of a rocky argument that seemed insincere at best.

That is not to say that Solicitor General Paul D. Clement didn't have some hurdles in his own oral argument—none more frustrating than arguing for a broader reading of the statute than Chief Justice John Roberts and Justice Stephen Breyer had understood from Petitioner's own brief. But the government's argument seemed to have a firm foundation in facts, evidence and compelling interests, while Respondent's argument seemed more like a Hollywood script, filled with fantasy and hyperbole.

The facts are these: On April 26, 2004, Michael Williams posted a public message in an Internet chat room, which read, "Dad of toddler has 'good' pics of her an [sic] me for swap of your toddler pics, or live cam." A federal agent who was monitoring the forum responded to the message and engaged the individual in conversation. In one of his responses Williams said, "I've got hc [hard core] pictures of me and dau, and other guys . . . —do you??" Williams later sent seven nude images of actual minors, approximately 5–15 years old, exposing themselves and/or engaging in sexually explicit conduct.

Mr. Williams was charged with two counts of possession of child pornography and promoting and distributing child pornography. After reserving the right to bring this constitutional action, he pleaded guilty to both counts.

Challenges to the Law

The statute under which Mr. Williams was charged [the PROTECT Act of 2003] prohibits "knowingly . . . advertis[ing], promot[ing], present[ing], distribut[ing], or solicit[ing] . . . Any material or purported material in a manner that reflects the belief, or that is intended to cause another to believe, that the material or purported material" is illegal child pornography. He appealed his conviction, saying the statute is overly broad and impermissibly vague and thus facially unconstitutional.

His argument goes like this:

Imagine: you could have someone reviewing *American Beauty* or *Traffic*—both Hollywood movies with some objectionable adult content—saying the movies depicted child pornography. Whether that assertion is true or not, the person can be charged under this statute. So, clearly there is protected speech that is reached by this statute, and, therefore, it is too broad or at least impermissibly vague.

I know that common sense tells you that this law is obviously not aimed at movie reviewers but at people like Mr. Williams who would pander illegal child pornography, including depictions of their own children. But we are talking about lawyers here, and this is the Supreme Court after all, so bear with me.

Part of the test the court would use . . . requires them to think of a reasonable *person in the situation, not of some person somewhere in some extreme circumstance.*

Respondent's counsel even argued that this law would have a chilling effect on free speech and that people who wanted to speak out in relation to a movie would feel that they could not for fear of violating the law.

The Justices did not seem impressed with the argument. Justice Breyer, after several futile attempts to obtain an answer from Respondent's Counsel as to the Government's assertion that this type of material falls outside of the statute, said that the objective requirement of the statute would annul that line of reasoning.

Using a Reasonable Standard

Part of the test the court would use to evaluate the statute requires them to think of a *reasonable* person in the situation, not of some person somewhere in some extreme circumstance who might think that the reviewer of the film is actually promoting real illegal child pornography.

> *Justice Breyer*: I don't see under [the government's] interpretation how anyone could conceivably be prosecuted even if he's talking to a group who have never seen a movie. That isn't a reasonable group of people.

Justice David Souter pushed even further, casting doubt on whether it would be substantial, and therefore not overly broad, even if there was some protected speech left somewhere.

Respondent's Counsel kept arguing that the most egregious aspect of the law was that it punished the intent of distributing the purported illegal child pornography even if the person is lying and there is no real child pornography. That is clearly protected free speech in Respondent's view.

Justice Antonin Scalia responded to this with another question that went unanswered by counsel.

> *Justice Scalia*: I had thought that the purpose of the First Amendment was to protect speech that had some value and that the reason obscenity is excluded entirely from First Amendment protection is that it has no redeeming social value. What social value do you find in being able to lie about the content of what you're offering to somebody else? You say somehow if you're lying about it, oh, well, then the First Amendment protects that. I would think if you're lying about it, it is clearer than ever the First Amendment doesn't protect it. There is no social value in protecting lies.

Respondent's Argument Weakens

Respondent's Counsel seemed lost. . . . Puzzled. . . . Confused. At times it sounded like he wasn't sure what role the First

Amendment played in the case and argued more from the reasoning that the penalty was just too strict.

> *Justice Samuel Alito*: And you think that's protected by the First Amendment? Asking someone for child pornography is protected?

> *Respondent's Counsel*: First of all, it may not be protected by the First Amendment, but it shouldn't be captured by this statute, which puts that 17-year-old in jail for 5–20 years.

> *Justice Ruth Bader Ginsburg*: The only thing that limits the statute is the First Amendment. What else—you say it may not be covered by the First Amendment. What else gives you a right to challenge the statute?

But the most frustrating thing about these types of cases at the Supreme Court is that the facts of the case at hand seem to get lost in extreme hypotheticals, theories and dreams in a far-off land. So it was a breath of fresh air when Justice Anthony Kennedy tried to put this case into perspective.

> *Justice Kennedy*: Your client here falls within none of these examples. He was convicted of having what everyone recognizes as not only child pornography but involving a very small child. And he knew what it was. And he—and he conveyed that belief. Given the fact that it would appear that child pornography is a growing problem, a serious problem on the Internet, maybe we should examine the overbreadth rule and just say that your client cannot make this challenge.

Not Enough Specifics

Although those are the facts of the case, challenges brought to the Supreme Court in these types of cases are heavily based on examples that have no meaning in the real world—hypotheticals, yes, but if you ask for concrete, real world examples, well, there are none.

Justice Ginsburg: I asked you have there been such cases? A lot of states have pandering laws now, and is the case that you posit a case that has occurred in any of those states?

Respondent's Counsel: Your Honor, I cannot cite a specific example, but. . . .

You get the picture.

If we are sincere in looking at the statute at hand and the facts presented by this case, there should be no question that there is no violation of the First Amendment right to free speech here. After all, the material at issue is illegal child pornography. The mere possession of it is a violation of the law. That was not challenged in this case.

It is clear that the federal government has a compelling interest in protecting children, and the statute goes after individuals with a specific intent to pander the material. A law that protects children in such a significant way should not be struck down simply because there might be one person somewhere in Fantasyland that, given the right circumstances, might say that it violates their free speech. That is nonsense.

7

The I.T. Industry Is Helping to Combat Child Pornography

John Foley

John Foley has written about networking, databases, operating systems, and other technology-related issues for Information-Week *since 1995. In March 2005, he was named editor of the magazine.*

The same technological advances that are improving the lives of today's young Americans are also being used to harm them through child pornography that is distributed more and more easily and broadly via the Internet. Fortunately, the technology industry is facing this problem head-on. Microsoft is trying to design Windows in a way that is resistant to storing child pornography. Other companies like Sun Microsystems, America Online, and Yahoo are also putting valuable resources into finding solutions to the problem. Law enforcement agencies have been able to track down pornography perpetrators using simple search engines like Google. They also have targeted Internet billing companies that pornographers use to collect money from subscribers, as well as hosting companies whose records have led them to the subscribers themselves. Such investigations demonstrate the increasingly prominent role played by technology, and technology professionals, in the fight against child pornography.

For years, carefully trained volunteers with Wired Kids Inc., a nonprofit organization devoted to online consumer safety, scoured the Web in search of child pornography. They

John Foley, "Technology and the Fight Against Child Porn," *InformationWeek*, February 14, 2005, p. 30–34. Copyright 2005 by CMP Media LLC, 600 Community Drive, Manhasset, NY 11030, USA. Reproduced by permission.

frequently found the illicit images and videos, and passed tips to law-enforcement personnel about the Web sites and chat rooms where they're exchanged. All too often, however, nothing happened. Frustrated that the group's efforts were wasted, Wired Kids' executive director and founder, Parry Aftab, has decided to pull back from the gumshoe work of proactively seeking child pornography and concentrate instead on public education and awareness. "The magnitude of the problem is so big that law enforcement can no longer even put a dent in it," Aftab says. "I'm tired of having people work and nothing happen."

The statistics bear out Aftab's concern. The National Center for Missing and Exploited Children's CyberTipline logged a 39% increase in reports of possession, creation, or distribution of child pornography in 2004, the seventh consecutive year child-pornography incidents have trended upward since the federally funded group set up its 24-hour hot line in 1998. "The problem is getting bigger," says Staca Urie, a supervisor with the center.

Ironically, the proliferation of child pornography is fueled by the same trend that's enriching the lives of children around the world: advances in computer technology and the global reach of the Web. In the same way that spam is an unwanted side effect of online correspondence, the widespread distribution of child pornography is an ugly by-product of digital technology. Encryption, key-chain storage devices, peer-to-peer networks, and Internet relay chat are used by child pornographers and pedophiles to correspond and share their illegal content with stomach-turning efficiency.

That makes child pornography a problem the technology industry can't ignore—and it isn't. Microsoft, for instance, is investigating whether Windows can be designed to resist storing child pornography. Computer Associates, Sun Microsystems, and other vendors contribute resources to the National Center for Missing and Exploited Children. And America Online and Yahoo both put "a tremendous amount of time and expertise into solving this problem," says Aftab, who also writes a column for *InformationWeek*. . . .

What's more, as the problem grows, so do the chances that IT departments will have to deal with it. According to the National Conference of State Legislators, which provides research to state policy-makers, at least four states—Arkansas, Missouri, South Carolina, and South Dakota—have enacted laws that require IT technicians to report suspected child pornography if they encounter it in the course of their work, and Oklahoma has drafted a similar bill. "There are a lot of corporations that learn about this stuff" by finding it on company computers, Aftab says. Products like Secure Computing Corp.'s SmartFilter let system administrators investigate, by content category, the Web pages visited by employees, with child pornography in the "extreme" category.

Law Enforcement's Strides

Law-enforcement agencies around the world are trying hard to track down the perpetrators. The Department of Homeland Security's U.S. Immigration and Customs Enforcement, the FBI, the Internal Revenue Service, the U.S. Postal Inspection Service, state-level Internet Crimes Against Children task forces, and officials in other countries collaborate on child-pornography investigations. Interpol and the International Center for Missing and Exploited Children, with $1 million in funding from Microsoft and philanthropist Sheila Johnson, are hosting a series of seminars in Europe, Asia, and Africa to train police in what to do.

One of the most successful crackdowns to date, known as the Falcon case, has resulted in more than 1,000 arrests in 13 countries, and the two-year pursuit isn't over. It was launched in February 2003, when Immigration and Customs Enforcement agents, using nothing more than PCs and Google Inc.'s search engine, quickly found their way to Web sites that charged from $49.95 to $79.95 per month for access to databases full of child pornography. "It's really, really easy," Immigration supervisory special agent Susan Cantor says. "We were immediately brought to those sites."

Rather than target just the Web-site operators, investigators decided to go after the Internet billing company that kept them in business, Regpay Co. Ltd., in Minsk, Belarus, and Connections USA Inc., a credit-card processor in Fort Lauderdale, Fla. After being extradited from other countries in Europe, where they were lured by investigators, three Regpay officials now sit in New Jersey jails facing charges of online child pornography and money laundering. Their trial in U.S. federal court is scheduled to begin next month [March 2005]. The president of Connections USA will be tried there, too.

A crackdown on the use of peer-to-peer file-sharing networks for child pornography . . . resulted in hundreds of searches and dozens of arrests.

A Vast Infrastructure

The Falcon case illustrates the international nature of the child-porn infrastructure. The IP addresses of the child-porn sites led investigators to servers operated by Rackspace Managed Hosting, based in San Antonio, Texas. Regpay was a Rackspace customer; Rackspace itself has not been implicated. Using search warrants, investigators obtained copies of the hard drives on those servers, and they hit the jackpot: The electronic records of 100,000 transactions conducted in the first six months of 2003, including credit-card information and other data that could be traced back to individual subscribers. "That's where we turned over the leaves," Cantor says.

In tracking down individual consumers of the child pornography, Falcon investigators put a priority on going after those who are in frequent contact with children, including a grade-school teacher, a pediatrician, a minister at an all-girls school, and a camp counselor. The latest suspect: a high-school social-studies teacher in Buffalo, N.Y., arrested Feb. 3 [2005] and alleged to have stored more than 400 child-porn images on his home computer. There are other reasons for child-porn distributors and consumers to look over their shoulders. Last spring, federal and state law-enforcement agencies announced a crackdown on the use of peer-to-peer file-sharing networks for child pornography that, at the time, had already resulted in hundreds of searches and dozens of arrests.

Despite such signs of progress, Aftab isn't alone in worrying it's not enough. "The problem is that as law enforcement increases the number of cases, it's increasing in a linear fashion, whereas the problem is exploding in an exponential way," says Robert Flores, administrator of the Justice Department's Office of Juvenile Justice and Delinquency Prevention.

There's also growing concern that the public is becoming desensitized to the issue of child pornography, as evidenced by incidents involving teenagers who create and share sexually explicit images of themselves or other teens that fit the definition of child pornography. "Kids are producing child porn and selling it," Aftab says. "It's crossed the line from the most contraband and heinous of all content to something everyone has seen or think they've seen."

Being Proactive Is Key

What can be done? Aftab and others say an increased emphasis on education and awareness is the next step. Wired Kids plans to merge its operations with Safeguarding Our Children—United Mothers . . . , a nonprofit organization also dedicated to child safety, and the combined group will focus on child-protection and cybersafety awareness and education.

The Justice Department plans to step up its messaging, too. "We want to start to educate kids about the danger of that whole industry, that it's not a benign thing," Flores says.

"Once you get sucked in, all sorts of things can happen." Among the associated risks are online enticement, sexual molestation, and child prostitution.

Industry groups representing peer-to-peer companies, under pressure to curb the use of their products for child pornography, have joined the fight. "We can and are playing a role in the education process and even in facilitating law enforcement," says Adam Eisgrau, executive director of Peer-to-Peer United.

Technology plays an increasingly important role in criminal investigations.

Private-sector companies are getting more proactive. One of the reasons the number of reports to the National Center for Missing and Exploited Children's hot line has jumped is that Internet service providers, in compliance with federal law, are reporting suspicious activity in greater numbers. And Immigration agent Cantor credits Visa and MasterCard with helping in the Falcon case. "The unfortunate reality of this business is they're very persistent," says a spokeswoman for Visa International, which uses a brand-protection service from NameProtect Inc. to identify Web sites that accept Visa cards as payment for child pornography and then reports those sites to law-enforcement agencies. "The site will shut down in one place then reopen in another. The problem doesn't go away."

Most companies monitor employee use of the Internet, some more strictly than others. At ATF Inc. "objectionable sites and/or material accessed from the work environment are cause for disciplinary action up to and including dismissal," says Gerald Spering, director of IT at the automotive-parts maker, in an E-mail. ATF uses Internet-monitoring tools "to try to protect employees from exposure to" such content,

Spering says, but he points out that it's more difficult to control what mobile workers such as salespeople access from the road with portable PCs.

Using Technology to Crack Networks

Technology plays an increasingly important role in criminal investigations. Microsoft has been working with law enforcement in Canada for more than a year to build a database to be used for child-porn investigative work. The soon-to-launch Child Exploitation Tracking System will make it possible for Canadian police to share case information in real time and map out relationships between people, connecting the dots among the shady characters who distribute and access child porn. But it's on Microsoft's Redmond, Wash., campus where some of the most interesting and potentially controversial work is under way. Developers there are considering ways to build into the Windows environment functionality that resists child pornography. "We are working internally to create products which are not going to be susceptible to that kind of misuse," says Rich LaMagna, director of worldwide digital integrity investigations and law-enforcement outreach for Microsoft.

It's unclear how far along Microsoft has gotten, but Hemanshu Nigam, a Microsoft lawyer whose background includes investigating child pornography at the Justice Department, has begun working directly with the Windows development group. Microsoft researchers also are exploring ways to determine whether a suspected child-porn image is authentic or a doctored-up digital composite.

Innovative uses of technology can make a difference. On Feb. 3 [2005], Toronto police released digital photos found on the Internet in hopes that the public might provide information on their origin. The image of the victim, a young girl, had been digitally erased from the pictures so that only the backgrounds could be seen. Police were hoping that someone might recognize the locations where the photos were taken, even though they were a couple of years old. Within hours, police got the lead they were hoping for when they learned that the pictures were taken at Walt Disney World in Florida, providing an extremely important clue in the case.

It's small victories like this that give child-protection advocates hope, despite the ever-expanding scope of this terrible trend. "We want to attack it at all levels, the supply and the demand," Immigration agent Cantor says. The mother of three adds, "I take it very personally."

8

Peer-to-Peer File-Sharing Facilitates the Dissemination of Child Pornography

Linda D. Koontz

Linda D. Koontz is director of information technology in the U.S. Government Accountability Office (GAO).

While the Internet has provided citizens with a number of new advantages and opportunities, it has also made pornographic images much easier to distribute and retrieve. In particular, peer-to-peer file-sharing software, which allows users to directly access files on other computers, greatly facilitates the retrieval of such images, even when it is not intentional. A 2004 search on KaZaA, one of the most popular file-sharing programs, revealed just how easy it is to access child pornography when using search words commonly associated with child pornography on such programs. Even when using innocuous search terms frequently used by young people, 49 percent of the resulting images were classified as pornography. This raises serious concerns about the likelihood of young people, who commonly use such programs for sharing music, being exposed to child pornographic images inadvertently. Fortunately, law enforcement is beginning to focus its resources on targeting such file-sharing programs as major sources of child pornography.

Linda D. Koontz, Testimony before "Online Pornography: Closing the Door on Pervasive Smut" hearing, *The House Committee on Energy and Commerce*, May 6, 2004. Reproduced by permission.

In recent years, child pornography has become increasingly available as it has migrated from magazines, photographs, and videos to the World Wide Web. As you know, a great strength of the Internet is that it includes a wide range of search and retrieval technologies that make finding information fast and easy. However, this capability also makes it easy to access, disseminate, and trade pornographic images and videos, including child pornography. As a result, child pornography has become accessible through Web sites, chat rooms, newsgroups, and the increasingly popular peer-to-peer technology, a form of networking that allows direct communication between computer users so that they can access and share each other's files (including images, video, and software).

My testimony today is based on our report on the availability of child pornography on peer-to-peer networks. As requested, I will summarize the results of our work to determine

- the ease of access to child pornography on peer-to-peer networks;

- the risk of inadvertent exposure of juvenile users of peer-to-peer networks to pornography, including child pornography; and

- the extent of federal law enforcement resources available for combating child pornography on peer-to-peer networks.

It is easy to access and download child pornography over peer-to-peer networks. We used KaZaA, a popular peer-to-peer file-sharing program, to search for image files, using 12 keywords known to be associated with child pornography on the Internet. Of 1,286 items identified in our search, about 42 percent were associated with child pornography images. The remaining items included 34 percent classified as adult pornography and 24 percent as nonpornographic. In another Ka-

ZaA search, the Customs CyberSmuggling Center used three keywords to search for and download child pornography image files. This search identified 341 image files, of which about 44 percent were classified as child pornography and 29 percent as adult pornography. The remaining images were classified as child erotica (13 percent) or other (nonpornographic) images (14 percent). These results are consistent with observations of the National Center for Missing and Exploited Children, which has stated that peer-to-peer technology is increasingly popular for the dissemination of child pornography. Since 2001, when the center began to track reports of child pornography on peer-to-peer networks, such reports have increased more than five-fold—from 156 in 2001 to 840 in 2003.

Pornographic Images Are Prevalent

When searching and downloading images on peer-to-peer networks, juvenile users can be inadvertently exposed to pornography, including child pornography. In searches on innocuous keywords likely to be used by juveniles, we obtained images that included a high proportion of pornography: in our searches, the retrieved images included adult pornography (34 percent), cartoon pornography (14 percent), and child pornography (1 percent); another 7 percent of the images were classified as child erotica.

We could not quantify the extent of federal law enforcement resources available for combating child pornography on peer-to-peer networks. Law enforcement agencies that work to combat child exploitation and child pornography do not track their resource use according to specific Internet technologies. However, law enforcement officials told us that, as they receive more tips concerning child pornography on peer-to-peer networks, they are focusing more resources in this area.

Child pornography is prohibited by federal statutes, which provide for civil and criminal penalties for its production, advertising, possession, receipt, distribution, and sale. Defined by statute as the visual depiction of a minor—a person under 18 years of age—engaged in sexually explicit conduct, child pornography is unprotected by the First Amendment, as it is intrinsically related to the sexual abuse of children.

In the Child Pornography Prevention Act of 1996, Congress sought to prohibit images that are or appear to be "of a minor engaging in sexually explicit conduct" or are "advertised, promoted, presented, described, or distributed in such a manner that conveys the impression that the material is or contains a visual depiction of a minor engaging in sexually explicit conduct." In 2002, the Supreme Court struck down this legislative attempt to ban "virtual" child pornography in *Ashcroft v. The Free Speech Coalition,* ruling that the expansion of the act to material that did not involve and thus harm actual children in its creation is an unconstitutional violation of free speech rights. According to government officials, this ruling may increase the difficulty of prosecuting those who produce and possess child pornography. Defendants may claim that pornographic images are of "virtual" children, thus requiring the government to establish that the children shown in these digital images are real. [In 2003], Congress enacted the PROTECT Act, which attempts to address the constitutional issues raised in The Free Speech Coalition decision.

Among the principal channels for the distribution of child pornography are commercial Web sites, Usenet newsgroups, and peer-to-peer networks.

The Internet Is Now the Principal Tool for Exchanging Child Pornography

Historically, pornography, including child pornography, tended to be found mainly in photographs, magazines, and videos. With the advent of the Internet, however, both the volume and the nature of available child pornography have changed significantly. The rapid expansion of the Internet and its technologies, the increased availability of broadband Internet services, advances in digital imaging technologies, and the availability of powerful digital graphic programs have led to a proliferation of child pornography on the Internet.

According to experts, pornographers have traditionally exploited—and sometimes pioneered—emerging communication technologies—from the dial-in bulletin board systems of the 1970s to the World Wide Web—to access, trade, and distribute pornography, including child pornography. Today, child pornography is available through virtually every Internet technology. . . .

Among the principal channels for the distribution of child pornography are commercial Web sites, Usenet newsgroups, and peer-to-peer networks.

Web sites. According to recent estimates, there are about 400,000 commercial pornography Web sites worldwide, with some of the sites selling pornographic images of children. The child pornography trade on the Internet is not only profitable, it has a worldwide reach: recently a child pornography ring was uncovered that included a Texas-based firm providing credit card billing and password access services for one Russian and two Indonesian child pornography Web sites. According to the U.S. Postal Inspection Service, the ring grossed as much as $1.4 million in just 1 month selling child pornography to paying customers.

Usenet. Usenet newsgroups also provide access to pornography, with several of the image-oriented newsgroups being focused on child erotica and child pornography. These newsgroups are frequently used by commercial pornographers who post "free" images to advertise adult and child pornography available for a fee from their Web sites.

Peer-to-peer networks. Although peer-to-peer file-sharing programs are largely known for the extensive sharing of copyrighted digital music, they are emerging as a conduit for the sharing of pornographic images and videos, including child pornography. In a recent study by congressional staff, a single search for the term "porn" using a file-sharing program yielded over 25,000 files. In another study, focused on the availability of pornographic video files on peer-to-peer sharing networks, a sample of 507 pornographic video files retrieved with a file-sharing program included about 3.7 percent child pornography videos. . . .

Peer-to-Peer Applications Provide Easy Access to Child Pornography

Child pornography is easily shared and accessed through peer-to-peer file-sharing programs. Our analysis of 1,286 titles and file names identified through KaZaA searches on 12 keywords showed that 543 (about 42 percent) of the images had titles and file names associated with child pornography images. Of the remaining files, 34 percent were classified as adult pornography, and 24 percent as nonpornographic. No files were downloaded for this analysis.

Juvenile users of peer-to-peer networks face a significant risk of inadvertent exposure to pornography when searching and downloading images.

The ease of access to child pornography files was further documented by retrieval and analysis of image files, performed on our behalf by the Customs CyberSmuggling Center. Using 3 of the 12 keywords that we used to document the availability of child pornography files, a CyberSmuggling Center analyst used KaZaA to search, identify, and download 305 files, including files containing multiple images and duplicates. The analyst was able to download 341 images from the 305 files identified through the KaZaA search.

The CyberSmuggling Center analysis of the 341 downloaded images showed that 149 (about 44 percent) of the downloaded images contained child pornography. The center classified the remaining images as child erotica (13 percent), adult pornography (29 percent), or nonpornographic (14 percent).

These results are consistent with the observations of NCMEC, which has stated that peer-to-peer technology is increasingly popular for the dissemination of child pornography. However, it is not the most prominent source for child pornography. Since 1998, most of the child pornography referred by the public to the CyberTipline was found on Internet Web sites. Since 1998, the center has received over 139,000 reports of child pornography, of which 76 percent concerned Web sites, and only 1 percent concerned peer-to-peer networks. Web site referrals have grown from about 1,400 in 1998 to over 45,000 in 2003—or about a thirty-two-fold increase. NCMEC did not track peer-to-peer referrals until 2001. Between 2001 and 2003, peer-to-peer referrals increased more than fivefold, from 156 to 840, reflecting the increased popularity of file-sharing programs. . . .

Juvenile Users May Be Inadvertently Exposed to Pornography

Juvenile users of peer-to-peer networks face a significant risk of inadvertent exposure to pornography when searching and downloading images. In a search using innocuous keywords likely to be used by juveniles searching peer-to-peer networks (such as names of popular singers, actors, and cartoon characters), almost half the images downloaded were classified as adult or cartoon pornography. Juvenile users also may be inadvertently exposed to child pornography through such searches, but the risk of such exposure is smaller than that of exposure to pornography in general.

To document the risk of inadvertent exposure of juvenile users to pornography, the Customs CyberSmuggling Center performed KaZaA searches using innocuous keywords likely to be used by juveniles. The center's image searches used three keywords representing the names of a popular female singer, child actors, and a cartoon character. A center analyst performed the search, retrieval, and analysis of the images. These searches produced 157 files, some of which were duplicates. From these 157 files, the analyst was able to download 177 images.

Our analysis of the CyberSmuggling Center's classification of the 177 downloaded images determined that 61 images contained adult pornography (34 percent), 24 images consisted of cartoon pornography (14 percent), 13 images contained child erotica (7 percent), and 2 images (1 percent) contained child pornography. The remaining 77 images were classified as nonpornographic.

The increase in reports of child pornography on peer-to-peer networks suggests that this problem is increasing.

Because law enforcement agencies do not track the resources dedicated to specific technologies used to access and download child pornography on the Internet, we were unable to quantify the resources devoted to investigations concerning peer-to-peer networks. These agencies (including the FBI, CEOS, and Customs) do devote significant resources to combating child exploitation and child pornography in general. Law enforcement officials told us, however, that as tips concerning child pornography on the peer-to-peer networks increase, they are beginning to focus more law enforcement resources on this issue. . . .

New Resources Focused on Peer-to-Peer Networks

An important new resource to facilitate the identification of the victims of child pornographers is the National Child Victim Identification Program, run by the CyberSmuggling Center. This resource is a consolidated information system containing seized images that is designed to allow law enforcement officials to quickly identify and combat the current abuse of children associated with the production of child pornography. The system's database is being populated with all known and unique child pornographic images obtained from national and international law enforcement sources and from CyberTipline reports filed with NCMEC. It will initially hold over 100,000 images collected by federal law enforcement agencies from various sources, including old child pornography magazines. According to Customs officials, this information will help, among other things, to determine whether actual children were used to produce child pornography images by matching them with images of children from magazines published before modern imaging technology was invented. Such evidence can be used to counter the assertion that only virtual children appear in certain images.

The system, which became operational in January 2003, is housed at the Customs CyberSmuggling Center and can be accessed remotely in "read only" format by the FBI, CEOS, the U.S. Postal Inspection Service, and NCMEC.

In summary, our work shows that child pornography as well as adult pornography is widely available and accessible on peer-to-peer networks. Even more disturbing, we found that peer-to-peer searches using seemingly innocent terms that clearly would be of interest to children produced a high proportion of pornographic material, including child pornography. The increase in reports of child pornography on peer-to-peer networks suggests that this problem is increasing. As a result, it will be important for law enforcement agencies to follow through on their plans to devote more resources to this technology and continue their efforts to develop effective strategies for addressing this problem.

9

The Threat of P2P File-Sharing for Child Pornography Is Exaggerated

Martin C. Lafferty

Martin C. Lafferty is chief executive officer of the Distributed Computing Industry Association.

The Internet has enabled citizens to connect with each other and share information and products with much greater ease and efficiency. Like other communication tools, it is a neutral technology in that it allows information exchange without distinguishing between types of information. This holds true for peer-to-peer file-sharing programs as well. However, some holders of content rights in the entertainment industry have not taken necessary precautions to protect their products from unauthorized copying and distribution. This irresponsibility has resulted in a disproportionate amount of pornographic content on the Internet. Contrary to the charge that file-sharing programs are used to distribute pornography more than other online technologies, several studies have shown that file-sharing software is not used any more for this purpose than other online environments such as Web sites. Nevertheless, most file-sharing software companies provide tools that allow parents to protect their children from exposure to pornographic content. The file-sharing industry is also working with law enforcement to help prosecute those who abuse this technology.

Martin C. Lafferty, Testimony before "Online Pornography: Closing the Door on Pervasive Smut" hearing, *The House Committee on Energy and Commerce*, May 6, 2004. Reproduced by permission.

The Internet is of immense value to society, particularly through its evolving and increasingly varied and decentralized usage as a tool for productivity, enabling exponentially faster and lower-cost means for connecting individuals globally, facilitating the exchange of all types of data, and creating a radically more efficient marketplace for commercial transactions. As with prior great communications inventions, Internet technology is neutral—facilitating communication without regard to whether content, or a transaction itself, may be deemed legal or illegal. Peer-to-peer file sharing, one of the newest advances of the Internet, is accomplished by client software search engines, returning queries from file directories, replacing costly and relatively slow centralized servers for both discovery and delivery of content, with an infinitely scalable number of participating PCs.

Some content rights holders in the entertainment industries have failed to stay current with technology advancements, and not taken reasonable precautions to protect their products from unauthorized copying and online redistribution. They have confused the public by selectively enforcing their rights, and have boycotted prospective and willing new distributors rather than licensing them. In the absence of their broadly authorizing mainstream content online and labeling it to protect users from inadvertent exposure to inappropriate material, as in offline media, the Internet overall has attracted a disproportionate amount of pornographic content, and adequate safeguards to consumers are for the most part not yet being provided.

Many computer users believe that the content they encounter on the Internet has been licensed and authorized as in other media that they routinely use such as television, radio, online subscription services, and various recording and playback devices. In Congressional hearings, computer users who have been sued by the record industry for alleged copyright infringement associated with online music redistribution, for example, have testified that they felt abused, prompting at least one U.S. parent to sue the RIAA [Recording Industry Association of America] under RICO [Racketeer Influenced and Corrupt Organizations Act] laws. Pornography on the Internet was initially limited by low bandwidth and limited sources. Those restrictions disappeared as modem speeds increased, broadband services proliferated, and pornography websites and chat-rooms multiplied. It has been challenging for Congress to balance consumer protection from undesired exposure with First Amendment rights issues. Credit-card routines intended to keep under-age users from accessing commercial pornography, for instance, have unfortunately proven easy to circumvent.

New Technology Poses New Challenges

More broadly, the dissemination of pornography, ranging from legal adult material to criminally obscene content, including the most pernicious category of child pornography, is facilitated online by such increasingly sophisticated electronic means as Internet browsers, search engines, e-mail, instant messaging, websites, peer-to-peer software, chat-rooms, and news groups, which technologies are now used regularly by tens of millions of U.S. citizens.

Such trafficking in pornography creates new challenges for content rights holders, computer manufacturers, software developers, and Internet service providers, to help protect minors from inadvertent exposure to such material online, and to educate the public, deter potential abusers, and enforce laws against dissemination of illegal material.

In light of these considerations, responsible content providers and legitimate technology companies have an increasing opportunity to collaborate to protect consumers from inadvertent exposure to undesirable and illegal content, through appropriate and applicable technical solutions, business practices, and educational programs. All stakeholders should be encouraged to explore such measures in good faith as well as adopting business models for legitimate content to be digitally distributed.

While the use of file-sharing software for the distribution of pornography is regrettable, it is less of a problem than activity in many other online environments.

Misconceptions About File-Sharing Programs

With the increasingly decentralized topology of the Internet, users themselves, including consumers of pornography, now serve frequently as the sources of content being entered into distribution, as well as being the recipients of it. Therefore, unfortunately, it is not remarkable that pornography is being distributed through many online technologies. As this activity has grown, it has become more difficult to obtain accurate data as to exact quantities and the precise nature of such content. Nevertheless, the following studies and reports demonstrate salient facts regarding such pornography on the Internet:

1. April 2004 reports from Websense, Nilesen/NetRatings, BigChampagne, and WebSpins indicate that pornography websites have increased seventeen-fold from 88,000 in 2000 to nearly 1.6 million today; 34 million people or about one-in-four U.S. Internet users visit them monthly, and 37 percent have visited a porn site at work; approximately 4.5 percent of downloaded peer-to-peer content is pornographic images, while approximately 19.3 percent is pornographic videos.

2. A November 2003 supplemental report from the General Accounting Office (GAO) to the Senate Judiciary Committee stated that the risks of inadvertent exposure to pornographic content using peer-to-peer file-sharing software are no greater than those posed by other uses

of the Internet (such as browsers, e-mail applications, instant messaging, websites, chat-rooms, news groups, or commercial search engines). Some 840 instances of reported child pornography were attributed to peer-to-peer software usage out of a 62,000 yearly total. 45,035 were on the Web, 12,043 were by e-mail, and 1,128 were on Usenet bulletin boards.

3. According to the National Center for Missing and Exploited Children (NCMEC), reported child pornography on peer-to-peer was down from 2% in 2002 to 1.4% in 2003, with the vast majority of the remaining 98%+ coming from websites and chat-rooms.

4. Further, as confirmed by DCIA [Distributed Computing Industry Association] member reports, unlike websites, there is no commercial child pornography distributed by means of peer-to-peer applications.

Thus, while the use of file-sharing software for the distribution of pornography is regrettable, it is less of a problem than activity in many other online environments. Finally, the leading file-sharing software suppliers provide tools enabling parents to protect their children from exposure to undesirable content. Users can choose options to block adult content, which is the default setting, add more keywords to be blocked, prevent all video and images from being downloaded, and password-protect their filter settings. While parental controls designed for search engines and other Internet applications, or distributed as stand-alone programs, may not automatically work with peer-to-peer software applications, the customized filtering solutions that have been incorporated in the leading file-sharing software programs are unexcelled in the levels of protection they provide and are setting the standard. Use of these tools and monitoring of use by parents and custodians must remain the primary protection of children from inappropriate Internet content.

File-Sharing Software Companies Are Helping, Not Hurting

Beyond the provision of parental control tools, leading peer-to-peer software companies have also worked cooperatively and proactively with law enforcement agencies on programs to facilitate prosecution of abusers of their technology, who attempt to distribute criminally obscene content. It should soon become apparent to distributors of such material that sharing it via peer-to-peer public folders is the best way to expose themselves to identification and prosecution. Leading peer-to-peer software companies are also working voluntarily on deterrence and education programs to further combat child pornography before enforcement actions are necessary. The DCIA, for example, is focusing its resources on a collaborative program to enable peer-to-peer users to recognize, report, and remove criminally obscene content from their computers.

> *Peer-to-peer software suppliers have affirmed their commitment to further reduce risks.*

While no amount of child pornography can be tolerated, the charge made by entertainment interests that peer-to-peer software exposes even children conducting unfiltered searches to a greater amount of pornography than those using an unfiltered Internet search engine is unsupported by evidence. Furthermore, in contradiction to these disingenuous allegations, using family filters included with leading peer-to-peer software applications set at the maximum level, in direct refutation of specific entertainment industry allegations, no files retrieved on searches for popular terms like "Britney," "Pokemon," and "Olsen Twins," will contain pornography, child pornography, or child erotica. By contrast, searching on these same terms using unfiltered search engines will yield many thousands of pornographic and criminally obscene results.

Entertainment industry comparisons of relative growth of pornographic files are also misleading. Their cited peer-to-peer figures typically correspond to the period of greatest growth in the consumer adoption of peer-to-peer software and actually represent a more than 50 percent reduction in the complaint-to-user ratio. By contrast, websites, chat-rooms, news groups and bulletin boards, already well established and relatively mature, represented more than 97 percent of reported incidents in this period. The record demonstrates that these issues have been and are being addressed, despite the greater challenges posed by a decentralized, user-generated file-sharing environment, resulting in a user experience comparable to, if not better than, that of surfing the Internet generally. While this concludes comments on the specific subject of this hearing, the following addresses other issues raised by the Subcommittee.

A Commitment to Reducing Risks

The innovative companies developing and distributing publicly accessible file-sharing software have also responded to other issues identified by Congress and through self-regulatory processes by making steady improvements. Additional relevant examples of their commendable track record include the integration of strong anti-virus software with peer-to-peer file-sharing applications, and the implementation of default settings and procedures to prevent inadvertent sharing of private or confidential data. Users can flexibly select the frequency of updating virus definitions; leading peer-to-peer companies promptly alert users of known attacks; and protected users help shield other users of file-sharing applications. With respect to safeguarding private information, current leading peer-to-peer software requires users to take multiple affirmative steps in order to share files that may include personal data. Peer-to-peer software suppliers have affirmed their commitment to further reduce risks and enhance both the safety and value of the user experience on behalf of their consumers and the public at large.

The DCIA is currently addressing spyware/adware, in part by working with two DCIA member companies in the Center for Democracy and Technology (CDT)–led Consumer Software Working Group (CSWG) since its inception. The DCIA also testified at the Federal Trade Commission's workshop in April 2004. At this event, it was made a matter of public record that leading peer-to-peer file-sharing suppliers, in addition to integrating powerful anti-virus software, now also certify that their programs are spyware-free. In addition, these suppliers offer consumers a choice of paid or ad-supported versions of their programs, with no pop-up ads appearing in the paid versions. Targeted advertising in the ad-supported versions collects no personally identifiable information, provides clear attribution as to its source, and is up to 40 times more efficient than traditional online advertising, meaning far fewer intrusions for users. Notifications are provided to consumers pre-installation, at download, and during operation; and the uninstallation of peer-to-peer programs, along with any associated advertising software, follows the same standard add/remove procedure as other legitimate applications. The DCIA readily acknowledges that more needs to be done to achieve its goal of establishing best practices in this area, and welcomes the opportunity to also coordinate with Congress on this issue.

The Real Solution

As noted earlier, however, the real obstacle to realization of the full potential of peer-to-peer technology is the refusal of key content owners to license their content for legitimate, paid distribution via peer-to-peer file sharing. In this regard, the DCIA commends the Subcommittee for scheduling a hearing on HR 107 "The Digital Media Consumers' Rights Act" on

May 12, 2004, in contrast to the Judiciary IP Subcommittee's introduction and reporting in a single day, with no hearing, of HR 4077, a measure that could criminalize millions of young Americans, given its vague negligence standards, for merely storing digital music on a networked device. The entertainment industries' strategy is to combine their refusal to license content with their aggressive attempt to demonize peer-to-peer technology, in an attempt to crush what they erroneously view as a threat to their interests. This is the same time-dishonored strategy they tried in the futile fight against photocopiers, video recorders, and many other innovations that have brought great benefits both to consumers and to the companies that at first opposed them. And it is *this* which deserves to be the subject of Congressional investigation.

The companies that develop and distribute peer-to-peer file-sharing software have made energetic efforts to license content . . . but have been consistently rebuffed.

DCIA members alone represent, with an average of 50 million licensed files now distributed monthly, the largest form of distribution of *legally* traded copyrighted music, movies, software, and video games on the Internet. This is accomplished primarily through agreements with small independent content suppliers, while the major studios and music labels continue their boycott of peer-to-peer. Nevertheless, licensed content distribution continues steadily to increase via peer-to-peer software programs. The challenges presented by digital content are indeed multifaceted, and no single response is sufficient. But among the different solutions that have been tried by the major music and movie rights holders, the most glaring omission is the most obvious one—providing consumers with legitimate choices in each digital medium, including peer-to-peer.

However, the continuing failure of the major labels and movie studios to license the peer-to-peer distribution channel exposes these users to potential lawsuits from the record industry for copyright infringement. This is the only unique threat that users of these applications face, and Congress should urge major labels and movie studios to swiftly license their content for all digital media, including peer-to-peer, in furtherance of the public interest.

The Entertainment Industry's Damaging Campaign

The full potential of peer-to-peer technology to benefit consumers has yet to be realized, and will not be achieved until content rights holders license their copyrighted works on a non-discriminatory basis for legitimate distribution by means of file-sharing applications. The ongoing boycott by major music labels and movie studios poses an increasingly serious threat, causing substantial damage to consumers, who are being harassed and threatened unnecessarily with lawsuits; to their shareholders, to whom they are denying a promising new revenue stream; and to content creators, particularly the independent labels and filmmakers seeking to monetize their copyrighted works using peer-to-peer distribution channels. The widespread availability of unprotected content from the majors severely disadvantages the independents from competing to sell their products using this most advanced and cost-effective distribution method.

The companies that develop and distribute peer-to-peer file-sharing software have made energetic efforts to license content from the major labels and movies studios, but have been consistently rebuffed, in what may constitute a collusive refusal to deal. Related to this, a technical amendment to HR 1417, providing a blanket anti-trust exemption for music in all digital media, was passed without hearing, resulting in a thousand-fold windfall benefit to record labels.

The current legitimate digital music marketplace is inadequate to properly serve consumers. Pricing at now licensed online music stores, for example, is maintained at artificially high levels so as not to compete with offline CD sales through an entrenched distribution infrastructure. Online store technology represents an older generation, less efficient centralized architecture. The quantity and quality of digital files made available for online sale are kept low so as not to be competitive with CD sales. Comparatively few users access these stores and fewer purchase files from them. The legitimate digital music marketplace needs to be expanded to encompass current and future technologies, including not only the latest Internet-based application, peer-to-peer file sharing, but also future technologies, with the requirement that music rights holders, and copyright holders generally, who wish to monetize their content in the digital realm, license it on nondiscriminatory terms for all digital media.

Motivated to Profit, Not Protect

Returning to the subject of this hearing, the entertainment industries are lobbying Congress with claims that file sharing is perilous to children and that peer-to-peer companies, though they have no control over user actions, should be responsible for the content of files some users independently share. At the same time, these entities intentionally and continuously bombard impressionable children and youth with shameful material. Major labels peddle hate-filled and reprehensible lyrics condoning, even promoting, criminal conduct, from drug trafficking and matricide to rape and theft. By their actions, these companies demonstrate they are motivated by a determination to protect their revenues and not by any tenderness for the young. Their conduct goes beyond unclean hands to a pernicious business model that should be reviewed by Congress as part of its media indecency initiative. Can it be that to incentivize the creation of a wide range of responsible entertainment we must at the same time make wealthy those bloodless cynics who shamelessly trade children's innocence for money and who undermine values such as faithfulness, work, sacrifice, selflessness, tolerance and self-discipline? Is this what the framers of the Constitution had in mind when they authorized the creation of copyright laws?

The entertainment industries' continuing emphasis on peer-to-peer pornography is unreflective of the much greater relative presence of pornography on the Web.

There can be no doubt that the ultimate motivation for such works is money. It cannot be supposed that any artist or corporate official has taken on partner abuse, child abandonment, robbery, date rape, homicide, or revenge as social missions that they would pursue absent the lure of dollars. Yes, such expressions are protected under the First Amendment, but where is the policy that says we must also facilitate the enrichment of their creators and promoters by imposing draconian measures on the citizenry? While this last line of argument takes us beyond the parameters of this hearing, the astonishing hypocrisy of the entertainment industries in this regard had to be pointed out.

Unproven Assertions Must Be Questioned

A primary reason the DCIA has felt compelled to comment at such length is that the entertainment industries' ongoing campaign to destroy the peer-to-peer software companies and to strangle file-sharing technology has gone largely unanswered. It is based upon the unproven assertion that labels and studios are suffering great economic damage through the copyright infringement of individual users. The DCIA's mission is to develop and promote the legitimate uses of P2P [peer-to-peer] functionality and to help foster business models that make partners, rather than litigants, of content owners, technology companies, Internet service providers, peer-to-peer software companies, and consumers.

The entertainment industries' continuing emphasis on peer-to-peer pornography is unreflective of the much greater relative presence of pornography on the Web, and of the much greater ease of transmitting pornography via e-mail and instant messaging attachments, not to mention the far greater risks of criminally obscene content available on websites, and of predatory dangers in chat-rooms. And it is so dismissive of peer-to-peer providers' efforts to work with law enforcement and to incorporate parental control software into their products that it starts to take on the character of a red herring. The inaccurate pornography charge too, is one of the pillars of the entertainment companies' platform for destroying the nascent distributed computing industry, oblivious to the damage wrought by their own intentional and shameful role.

Demand Content Licensing

Both copyright infringement and exposure of children to pornography are real problems, and we condemn them. However, we also encourage Congress to consider the possibility that the entertainment industries' ceaseless chant of piracy, and their unbalanced and diversionary claim of pornography, are not such issues as demand an inexorable tightening of the legislative screws on millions of Americans, young and old, by an angry Congress on behalf of unworthy supplicants. Instead, we commend to you the idea that these campaigns, on which so much money and so many words have been spent, are excuses that serve the purpose of shielding poor management from investor scrutiny, and of substituting for a lack of strategic business vision and for a lack of artistic creativity, and for an inability to learn from the lessons of the past regarding the development of earlier media distribution technologies.

How much more beneficial and constructive it would be for the United States and all of its citizens, and for the entertainment companies themselves and their shareholders, if as the next step in development of the new and rapidly changing decentralized digital distribution marketplace, Congress were to adopt an alternative along these lines: "To be effective on the date of initial publishing of a copyrighted work, any rights holder who wishes to monetize the digital redistribution of such work on the Internet and otherwise, shall be required to provide in advance terms and conditions on a non-discriminatory wholesale basis to all distributors, including software suppliers and individuals, who may wish to engage in such redistribution." Once the law has been modified in such a way to ensure that the "carrot" of legitimate licensed content redistribution can be supported given the realities of technical advancements now affecting the topology of the Internet itself, then the "stick" of enforcement could reasonably be revisited, with more appropriate requirements for commercial parties who may then be expected to bear increased responsibilities for protecting the new forms of commerce so enabled. These would logically include appropriate labeling and warnings for adult content, actions to combat criminally obscene content, and other measures to fully legitimize online entertainment distribution.

10

Internet Service Providers Should Be Mandated to Retain Subscriber Data

Alberto R. Gonzales

Alberto R. Gonzales was the 80th attorney general of the United States, serving between February 2005 and September 2007 under President George W. Bush.

The Internet is not just a tool for the mass dissemination and retrieval of child pornography; it also serves as a community for pornographers and pedophiles that validates and encourages their behavior. As such, consumers of pornographic images online often become producers of images as well, thereby increasing the sources of pornography and numbers of child victims. This vicious cycle of child pornography on the Internet cannot be tolerated. To stop it, law enforcement must have every tool at its disposal, including evidence of potential offenders' online activity that is usually held by Internet service providers (ISPs). Some ISPs, though, do not retain records of subscriber activity, which hinders law enforcement's capacity to prosecute offenders. A new piece of legislation being sent to Congress, the Child Pornography and Obscenity Prevention Amendments of 2006, will require providers to report any child pornography found on their systems and sanction those providers who fail to report it. This legislation should aid in law enforcement's prosecution of child pornographers, as well as decrease the chance of innocent Internet users inadvertently stumbling upon pornographic images.

Alberto R. Gonzales, Prepared remarks at the National Center for Missing and Exploited Children, in U.S. Department of Justice, April 20, 2006.

Sadly, the Internet age has created a vicious cycle in which child pornography continually becomes more widespread, more graphic, and more sadistic, using younger and younger children. . . . Let me explain a bit, because having the public understand it is critical to appreciating the present state of the problem.

At the most basic level, the Internet is used as a tool for sending and receiving large amounts of child pornography on a relatively anonymous basis. But the Internet has become more than just an expanding supply of images for pedophiles to gratify their urges.

Before the Internet, these pedophiles were isolated—unwelcome even in most adult bookstores. Through the Internet, they have found a community. Offenders can bond with each other, and the Internet acts as a tool for legitimizing and validating their behavior in their minds. It emboldens them.

And this is where the Internet's vicious cycle leads to the trends I mentioned above. The pedophiles seek to build larger collections of photographs and videos, as a license into their community. As they become de-sensitized to the images they have, they seek more graphic, more heinous, and more disturbing material.

At some point, the pedophiles meet strong incentives not just to collect images, but to produce new ones themselves. Part of it is the desire to see novel and more graphic images, with younger and younger children. And today's technology makes it easier and less costly for anyone to produce these images and distribute them widely.

The other incentive is that trading rules in parts of this community require that participants offer new pornographic images in order to get images from fellow users. Images of sexual abuse of children become something of a currency—a way to get more pictures. Collectors become producers, and to be in the club, they have to find a child to abuse. And they are driven by the desire for increasingly graphic images.

So the Internet just feeds a vicious cycle. It makes child pornography more accessible and validates the pedophiles' behavior in their minds, driving them to molest even more children and to make new and increasingly vulgar material.

New Forms of Abuse

The Internet has also fundamentally changed the type of victimization that children endure. Imagine a 10-year-old boy who is sexually abused by a family member. He will always wear the scars of that tragic moment. And stopping the abuse means uprooting the family, which further affects children.

And, because of the Internet and the trends it has caused, he will continue to be victimized in other ways. Pedophiles will often use the images of children as a tool to silence them or to blackmail them into more molestation or pornography—or worse yet, into the horrific trades of child trafficking and prostitution. And the boy will always know that the pictures of his very personal abuse are out there on the Internet, which leads to feelings of embarrassment and helplessness that cause an ongoing and cruel victimization.

Another trend we are seeing is the so-called "molestation on demand," where a pedophile molests a child and others watch live through streaming video. We saw that in Operation Hamlet [the 2002 bust of an international pedophile ring].

We cannot, and will not, tolerate those who seek to abuse or exploit our children.

A variation of the on-demand abuse was in *United States v. Mariscal.* We found that Mariscal had been traveling to Cuba and Ecuador over a seven-year period, taking orders from customers to produce child porn to the customers' liking. He would allow customers to write fantasy scripts, and then he would find poverty-stricken families and pay them to allow him to sexually abuse their children, some under the age of 12. And Mariscal would make between $600 and $1,000 per order. To make matters worse, Mariscal was HIV-positive. We caught him and his co-conspirators, and in September 2004 he was sentenced to a 100-year prison term.

I'd like to say that these kinds of criminal behaviors are isolated or rare. Sadly, they are not. It is not an exaggeration to say that we are in the midst of an epidemic in the production and trafficking of movies and images depicting the sexual abuse of children. Now, more than ever, we need to educate the public on the realities of the dangers posed by child sexual predators, abusers, and pornographers.

Utilizing All Resources

The question becomes how we, as a society, will respond. There can be only one answer: We cannot, and will not, tolerate those who seek to abuse or exploit our children.

President [George W.] Bush is absolutely committed to this cause. He has made my mission clear, stating, and I quote, "Anyone who targets a child for harm will be a primary target of law enforcement."

The failure of some Internet service providers to keep records has hampered our ability to conduct investigations in this area.

At the [Justice] Department, we are working more of these cases than ever before in the Child Exploitation and Obscenity Section, in the FBI's Innocent Images Unit, and in U.S. Attorneys Offices around the country. We are funding the Internet Crimes Against Children [ICAC] program, a successful network of 45 task forces that I know you all work with closely. Under President Bush the funding for the ICAC program has more than doubled, to over $14 million in fiscal year 2006.

On February 15 [2006]—following the President's directive to protect our children—I announced Project Safe

Childhood, an initiative aimed at combating the online exploitation and victimization of children.

Through Project Safe Childhood, we will build on our efforts in this area by making law enforcement at all levels more coordinated, better trained, and more involved. And we will use our federal resources at the Justice Department to make sure we find these criminals and keep them away from our kids.

We are moving closer to formally implementing Project Safe Childhood, after soliciting support and suggestions from a number of people and organizations, including the National Center. I intend to announce additional details next month [May 2006]. It is my hope that this new program will make a real difference in the lives of Americans, and especially our children.

Evidence Must Be Made Available

But in order for Project Safe Childhood to succeed, we have to make sure law enforcement has all the tools and information it needs to wage this battle. The investigation and prosecution of child predators depends critically on the availability of evidence that is often in the hands of Internet service providers. This evidence will be available for us to use only if the providers retain the records for a reasonable amount of time. Unfortunately, the failure of some Internet service providers to keep records has hampered our ability to conduct investigations in this area.

As a result, I have asked the appropriate experts at the Department to examine this issue and provide me with proposed recommendations. And I will reach out personally to the CEOs of the leading service providers, and to other industry leaders, to solicit their input and assistance. Record retention by Internet service providers consistent with the legitimate privacy rights of Americans is an issue that must be addressed.

I am also proud to announce today that the Administration will send to Congress a new piece of legislation, the Child Pornography and Obscenity Prevention Amendments of 2006. This legislation will help ensure that communications providers report the presence of child pornography on their systems by strengthening criminal penalties for failing to report it. It will also prevent people from inadvertently stumbling across pornographic images on the Internet. I hope Congress will take up this legislation promptly.

11

The Risks of Data Retention by ISPs Outweigh the Rewards

Center for Democracy and Technology

The Center for Democracy & Technology is an organization that seeks to preserve democracy and civil liberties in the realm of technology. In particular, it is concerned with protecting free expression and privacy in new media such as the Internet.

The attorney general has announced his intention to require that Internet service providers (ISPs) and others in the communications industry keep records of their subscribers' online activity. While the Center for Democracy and Technology fully supports law enforcement's efforts to crack down on child pornography, there remain serious doubts as to whether requiring data retention of ISPs would actually lead to more prosecutions of child pornographers. Further, such a requirement could prove harmful by threatening privacy and security, increasing costs, and decreasing effectiveness. Before passing a law that requires data retention, Congress must require the administration to demonstrate that the current data retention law is insufficient and how a new requirement would be more effective. It should also look at alternative measures that would help law enforcement efforts while still maintaining privacy and security.

The Attorney General and the FBI Director have said that Internet Service Providers [ISPs] and others should be required to maintain for some extended period of time data identifying their customers' online activity. Among the Mem-

Center for Democracy and Technology, "Mandatory Data Retention Poses Major Concerns, May Have Little Benefit," November 13, 2006. Reproduced by permission.

bers of Congress who have embraced the idea is Congresswoman Diana DeGette (D-CO), who introduced and then withdrew a proposal earlier this year [2006]. The Justice Department has had several meetings with industry representatives and privacy groups to discuss the concept of data retention legislation. The full scope of the mandate remains undefined, but it could encompass not only ISPs but also website operators, telephone companies, cable companies, wireless carriers, employers who provide employees with Internet access, hotels, libraries, universities, and WiFi hotspot providers.

During House Energy and Commerce Committee hearings on ISPs and child safety earlier this year, some ISP representatives testified that their companies always have retained, or had begun to retain, certain subscriber identifying information for extended periods of time in anticipation of—or perhaps to obviate—data retention legislation. For instance, Comcast announced that it would begin retaining IP [Internet Protocol] addresses assigned to its subscribers for 180 days instead of 31 days, which had been its policy. Earthlink stated that it retains "RADIUS [Remote Authentication Dial In User Service]" logs for several months in a "live," immediately accessible database and stores the logs off-site in an archived format for up to seven years.

CDT [Center for Democracy and Technology] has long been at the forefront of efforts to empower parents and other caretakers to protect children from offensive content and dangerous conduct online. We fully support the criminalization of child pornography and we believe that law enforcement agencies at the federal, state and local levels should be well-trained and have sufficient resources to pursue child pornography and abuse cases.

Small Benefits, Big Risks

For the reasons set out below, however, we seriously doubt whether a data retention requirement would be likely to contribute in a significant way to protecting children or fighting terrorism. Instead, a mandate would pose other risks that seem likely to outweigh any possible benefits, and it might actually harm, rather than enhance national security and law enforcement efforts to find child predators online. Indeed, data retention proposals raise serious concerns about privacy, security, cost, and effectiveness.

Data retention laws threaten personal privacy and pose a security risk.

Before Congress takes the radical step of enacting mandatory data retention legislation, it should require the administration to show how the existing data preservation law is insufficient, whether a data retention requirement is likely to be effective, the effect of a data retention requirement on personal privacy and data security, and what the costs associated with data retention would be for government and industry. At the very least, Congress should consider several alternatives and amendments to existing laws that would better focus law enforcement *and* protect data privacy and security.

CDT coordinates the Digital Privacy and Security Working Group (DPSWG), a forum for a wide range of computer and communications companies, trade associations, and public interest organizations interested in communications privacy and security issues. CDT has invited Department of Justice officials to meet with DPSWG to explore in greater detail the government's needs and industry's role in protecting children online. CDT believes that, before legislation is considered, all stakeholders need a better understanding of how the government conducts investigations related to child pornography, child exploitation and related offenses, including such questions as: What information is most relevant to the government's investigations? What are the current practices and experiences in storing and accessing that information?

What better ways might there be to get that information to the government? What are the technological tools available or in development to identify child pornography or situations of potential abuse? Until these questions are addressed, legislation is premature.

Core Concerns with Data Retention Legislation

Data retention laws threaten personal privacy and pose a security risk, at the very time the public is justifiably concerned about security and privacy online.

One of the best ways to protect privacy is to minimize the amount of data collected in the first place. A data retention law would undermine this important principle, resulting in the collection of large amounts of information that could be abused and misused.

Mandatory data retention laws will create large databases of information that trace personal contacts and relationships and will make subscribers' personal information vulnerable to hackers or accidental disclosure.

At a time when identity theft is a major concern and security vulnerabilities in the Internet have not been adequately addressed, data retention would aggravate the risk of data breaches and unauthorized use.

The Internet activity of Members of Congress, law enforcement officials and other government agencies would also get swept up in the proposed retention of Internet data. Retention, given the threat of unauthorized access, thus poses risks to law enforcement and to homeland and national security.

Laws Could Backfire

Data retention laws are likely to have only limited benefit and, in fact, could impede law enforcement's ability to track and apprehend criminals.

The current data preservation law is preferable to data retention because a data preservation request can specify exactly what information is needed for the investigation at hand. Data retention laws, on the other hand, take a "one-size-fits-all" approach that is unsuited to the dynamic nature of Internet investigations.

Criminals will always be able to thwart data retention laws by finding ways to prevent their data from being traced—using public facilities, using proxies and other anonymizing technology. A data retention law therefore would be most effective in capturing the data of innocent people, not criminals, and it could hurt law enforcement by driving criminals to use technologies that would render even existing data preservation laws ineffective.

Data retention laws are likely to be both over-inclusive and under-inclusive at the same time—forcing service providers to store multiple terabytes of useless information while possibly missing the information that would be useful in a particular investigation.

Retention of more data than is necessary to achieve law enforcement objectives will be counterproductive, drowning companies and investigators in irrelevant and potentially misleading information that will be very difficult to search or use.

Commercial ISPs would retain detailed records of all communications to, from and between members of police departments and the FBI. This data would be an attractive target to criminals and terrorist groups and would increase the risk of exposure of undercover investigators and confidential informants.

Data retention laws could prompt service providers to store data "off-shore," where it would be out of the immediate reach of law enforcement and where access would be subject to the laws of other countries, defeating the whole purpose of the mandate.

Mission Creep Potential

Data retention laws create the danger of mission creep.

The vast databases that ISPs and telecom providers will create could be tapped by law enforcement for other purposes unrelated to child porn investigations.

Service providers themselves might be tempted to use the stored information for a range of currently unanticipated purposes.

Data retention laws are unnecessary—authority already exists to preserve records.

Already, under current law, any governmental entity can require any service provider (telephone company, ISP, cable company, university) to immediately preserve any records in its possession for up to 90 days, renewable indefinitely.

Data preservation orders are mandatory—service providers must comply.

The Department of Justice and other law enforcement agencies have not effectively used the authority already at their disposal.

Data preservation orders do not require judicial approval and do not need to meet any evidentiary threshold.

There has been no showing that this "data preservation" authority is inadequate.

There is no showing that ISPs fail to cooperate with data preservation requests.

The Internet and telecommunications industry is committed to cooperating with law enforcement, but the DOJ [Department of Justice] and other law enforcement agencies have not effectively used the authority already at their disposal.

DOJ has failed to follow up on allegations of online child sexual abuse, but this has not been due to lack of evidence. Justin Berry, the now 19-year-old whose story in the *New York Times* triggered the current wave of concern, testified at length last summer before the House Commerce Committee about the failure of DOJ to follow up on information he provided to the Child Exploitation and Obscenity Section, including names, credit card numbers and computer IP addresses of approximately 1,500 people who paid to watch child pornography from his sites.

Privacy Issues

Proceeding with data retention would require a full-scale re-examination of data privacy laws.

The European Union enacted a data retention rule last year, but the EU also has detailed rules governing the privacy of electronic communications information in terms of both governmental access and corporate use and disclosure. The U.S. does not have a privacy law that adequately protects the data that would be collected and retained.

In particular, the Electronic Communications Privacy Act (ECPA) sets very low standards for governmental access to data and places no limits on the secondary use that ISPs can make of the non-content information they collect and maintain about their subscribers. Service providers can, unless they make a privacy promise to the contrary, disclose subscriber-identifying information for any purpose, except to a governmental entity, and government agencies can access the data without judicial approval. Mandating large-scale data retention would upset the balance in ECPA and would require a larger re-examination of how that law works.

A data retention database could serve as a honey pot for trial lawyers in civil cases.

Already, the vast majority of requests that ISPs and other online service providers receive for customer information come not from the government but from private litigants in divorce cases, copyright enforcement actions, and commercial lawsuits.

Whistleblowers and journalists also would be among those whose records could be subpoenaed.

Data retention laws undermine public trust in the Internet.

Subscribers are less likely to use services that compromise the privacy and security of their personal information. Because data retention would apply to all Internet services, most of the impact would fall on legitimate service providers. Ordinary users engaging in everyday activity might hesitate to use a range of online services.

A Rise in Costs

Data retention would be burdensome and costly.

Data retention laws would require investments in storage equipment and force ISPs to incur large annual operating costs. Companies would also incur the cost of hiring and training employees whose sole responsibility would be to conduct searches for and provide information to law enforcement and civil litigants. Training ISP employees in the proper handling and use of data would be essential to ensure admissibility of this data in court.

As one example, AOL UK estimated that its compliance with the EU data retention directive would cost at least $40 million to implement and another $14 million per year to maintain.

The costs associated with data retention would be passed on to consumers, inhibiting efforts to expand Internet access to poorer communities.

There are other, less burdensome but more effective measures that Congress, the Justice Department, and child protection advocates should consider.

Data retention laws could force websites that currently offer free content to the public to start charging fees for access to their sites and could put small ISPs out of business and discourage new entrants to market.

The potential costs will increase exponentially with the growth of the Internet and the inevitable cross-border requests pursuant to information-sharing treaties between the U.S. and other countries.

Possible Alternatives to Data Retention Legislation

There are other, less burdensome but more effective measures that Congress, the Justice Department, and child protection advocates should consider:

Allow the National Center for Missing and Exploited Children (NCMEC) to issue data preservation orders, or alternatively, require entities to retain information immediately upon making a referral to NCMEC under 42 USC §13032. (Currently, only government entities can issue data preservation orders under 18 USC §2703(f).) (Note that under current law, ISPs are permitted to disclose non-content information to NCMEC *without* any judicial process. See 18 USC §2702(c)(5).)

Place a federal prosecutor with authority to issue subpoenas at NCMEC so that information can be obtained immediately after service providers make referrals. This would assist law enforcement in obtaining the information it needs without having to wait for referrals from NCMEC.

Require companies to include IP address (and any available subscriber identifying information) in initial report to NCMEC under Section 13032 to expedite and facilitate investigations.

Increase resources for staffing and training of law enforcement and for necessary improvements to technical support and infrastructure.

Policy Issues Congress Must Consider Before It Legislates

While we remain opposed to mandatory data retention legislation, the following are some questions that should be addressed before Congress considers legislation.

What information should companies have to retain? Companies should not be forced to retain information that they don't already generate and save (for some period of time) for business purposes. The entities to be covered and the type of information to be retained would have to be very precisely and narrowly defined. It seems there is no reason, for example, to retain any information other than IP addresses assigned to customers.

What should be the standard for government access to the data? Transactional information related to Internet communications is currently available to the government with a subpoena or a National Security Letter, neither of which requires judicial approval. In the case of data retained for the benefit of the government, shouldn't the statute require the government to obtain at least a court order under 18 USC 2703(d) before getting access to the data? While IP addresses currently are available with a subpoena, Internet records like IP addresses are much more revealing than traditional subscriber identifying information, especially since they can be combined with other information routinely stored by search engines and content providers.

What obligations should ISPs have to maintain the integrity and security of the data?

Should ISPs be precluded from using retained information for secondary purposes without first obtaining customer consent? Should ISPs be allowed to use the information for *any* secondary purpose? Under current law, ISPs are permitted to use their customers' non-content information and to disclose it to "any person other than a governmental entity," meaning

that ISPs could lawfully use or disclose any information retained pursuant to the data retention mandate to any non-
governmental entity.

Should legislation provide a statutory remedy—such as an
exclusionary rule—to defendants whose electronic communications or records were obtained in violation of the statute?
Similarly, should legislation impose penalties on those who
make improper requests for or misuse data obtained under
the mandate?

---

*The government should only get access to the informa-
tion relevant to a particular, ongoing investigation.*

Should a data retention mandate be coupled with a data
destruction mandate? Should the government be required to
delete information it obtains pursuant to the mandate, after
such information is no longer needed for the investigation for
which it was obtained?

What types of Internet access providers will the statute
cover? Will the coverage be limited to actual network providers (Earthlink, AOL, etc.)? Extending coverage to small access
providers like libraries, coffee shops, hotels and other WiFi
hotspots would add huge costs with little benefit.

Will government access to the data be limited to certain
investigatory purposes? Because the justification put forth so
far has focused on child pornography, the government should
not have access to the data for other purposes without Congressional authorization, except when emergencies involving
immediate danger of death or serious physical injury to any
person justify disclosure of the information. Furthermore, the
government should be prohibited from using this information
for data mining or other predictive purposes. The government
should only get access to the information relevant to a particular, ongoing investigation.

What kind of oversight is appropriate? Is a sunset provision appropriate? Congress should receive periodic reports showing the number of requests made, the number and types of investigations in which the information was used, and the effectiveness of the data retention mandate in combating child porn.

In order to ensure public confidence and government accountability and to deter abuse, should law enforcement be required to notify the persons whose information it obtains? Legislation could require after-the-fact notice, unless a senior law enforcement officer certifies that such notice would jeopardize an ongoing investigation.

12

Journalists Need an Exemption to Report on Child Pornography

Debbie Nathan

Debbie Nathan is a journalist who writes about immigration and sexual politics. Her work has appeared in the Village Voice, The Nation, The New York Times, *and other publications.*

Recently, Bernie Ward, a liberal talk show host known for criticizing the George W. Bush administration, was indicted on federal child pornography charges. Ward was researching child pornography for a book, and evidence shows the government was aware of this. This case is very similar to the case of Larry Matthews, a radio reporter in Washington, D.C., who was brought up on charges in the late 1990s after acquiring some child pornography for a story. At the same time that both of these men were brought up on charges when the government clearly recognized their journalistic intent, The New York Times *reporter Kurt Eichenwald was left alone. It is clear that Eichenwald broke the same laws that Ward and Matthews did; in fact, the extent of his dealings in child pornography is truly suspicious. Yet Eichenwald also turned in state's evidence against pornographers he met, and he also testified in Congressional hearings. The fact that the government picks and chooses who to prosecute, based on whom they deem as allies, leaves journalists covering child pornography utterly vulnerable to prosecution. To avoid this, there should be some sort of First Amendment exemption that*

Debbie Nathan, "The Curious Indictment of Bernie Ward: The Perils of Journalism and Child Porn," *CounterPunch*, December 10, 2007. Reproduced by permission.

would allow reporters to properly cover child pornography without the risk of indictment.

Bernie Ward, a San Francisco-based liberal talk show host, was indicted [December 6, 2007] on federal child pornography charges. His is the second such indictment brought against a media figure who then claimed he had the porn merely to do research and reporting. Meanwhile, a third journalist, a former *New York Times* reporter who engaged in similar behavior, has not been indicted. The inconsistency suggests that the government chooses whom to go after and whom to leave alone. And it makes clear that the media needs a First Amendment exemption or license allowing reporters to examine child pornography legally.

Before his indictment on December 6, Ward—who is 56 and married with four children—had two programs on San Francisco's KGO-AM radio. One was a nightly political and news talk show; the other aired weekly and dealt with religion. In the 1980s Ward was an award-winning general assignment and political reporter at KGO. He is also known for conducting major fundraising drives for Bay Area non-profits that help the homeless and others in need. From 1982 to 1985 he worked for then-Rep. Barbara Boxer as her chief legislative assistant. On KGO and on national talk shows, he strenuously opposed the war in Iraq and other Bush Adminstration policies. KGO billed him as "The Lion of the Left." Following his indictment, he has been put on leave from the station.

Ward's lawyer, Doron Weinberg, told the *San Francisco Chronicle* that Ward accessed and distributed only a small amount of child pornography three years ago, for research he was doing to write a book about hypocrisy in America. The *Chronicle* quoted sources familiar with the case saying that "authorities noted that Ward was monitored as he went on a chat room and sent and received images."

Indictment papers released on Friday support Ward's claim that the government was involved in the case as early as 2004 but waited years to indict.

A Comparable Case

Ward's case is strikingly similar to that of Larry Matthews, a media figure who faced child porn charges in the late 1990s. Matthews was a Washington DC-area radio reporter in his late 50s. He had won press awards and was known for covering social issues, including the problem of internet child porn. When arrested, he said he had acquired illegal material because he was impersonating a pedophile in order to do another story.

The government countered that Matthews had no notes or story assignment from a media outlet. The ACLU [American Civil Liberties Union], National Public Radio, and other press and First Amendment organizations spoke out for him and filed supporting legal briefs. But an appellate court later ruled that journalists have no right to acquire or distribute child pornography while doing research. Matthews was convicted and served several months in a halfway house.

A reporter deliberately researching child pornography would . . . hardly qualify for "forgiveness" under [U.S. Code] 2252.

If convicted, San Francisco's Ward faces a maximum 15 years for each of three criminal counts.

"The government knows that Bernie was doing this for an investigation he was doing for a book," the *Chronicle* quoted attorney Weinberg saying. "But the government believes he violated the letter of the law, and they have gone ahead and prosecuted him. . . . The fact that these events happened three years ago—and they are just being prosecuted—shows the fact that nobody believes that he is a child predator." The *Exam-*

iner seemingly attempted to explain how Ward could have avoided prosecution by citing a federal law—which the paper mistakenly said "forgives" possession of three child pornography images if they are destroyed and promptly reported to authorities. In fact, that statute, which is part of U.S. Code 2252, allows only two images. And some legal scholars interpret 2252 as "forgiving" someone only if he or she came to possess child porn by accident rather than intentionally. A reporter deliberately researching child pornography would thus hardly qualify for "forgiveness" under 2252. In addition, the law is merely an "affirmative defense." To exercise it, one would have to first be indicted. There is no case law indicating that any journalist has ever used 2252 to justify their work after being charged with possession or distribution of child porn.

Eichenwald Exempted

However, the statute was cited in August 2006 by the *New York Times*. Kurt Eichenwald, then a *Times* reporter, said he accidentally accessed a few illegal images while doing month's-long reporting on Internet child pornography. In a sidebar to one of Eichenwald's articles, the *Times* said that a law—presumably 2252—excused the reporter's encounter with the illegal material. But Eichenwald's published work implied he had accessed far more than two images.

Further, Eichenwald in 2005 obtained and used administrative sign-on privileges to explore a commercial porn website containing images of a 14-year-old boy masturbating. Eichenwald went on to write a major *Times* story based on reporting he did about this site and the people who ran it.

Eichenwald took the young man who ran the site to federal authorities, where he turned state's evidence against his business partners in exchange for prosecutorial immunity. As a result, four people were arrested and convicted. Eichenwald's work also led to Congressional hearings—at which he testified—where witnesses made unsubstantiated claims about the prevalence of Internet child predators and pornography. Those hearings were a run-up to passage of the 2006 Adam Walsh Act. It requires states to put children and very low-level offenders, such as public urinators and people caught with small amounts of child porn, on sexual offender registries for years—a policy that has since been condemned by Human Rights Watch. Since 9/11, the government has used unsubstantiated claims about the extent of child pornography to defend sections of the Patriot Act which intrude on internet privacy.

Inconsistent Enforcement

Eichenwald claimed he became involved with child pornography to find out about the problem. In some instances, he did not tell *Times* editors what he was doing. Later expose of his activities provoked intense controversy in the media world, and currently he is not working as a journalist. However, he has not been criminally prosecuted. . . .

Journalists need some kind of system or First Amendment permit to allow them to do their reporting.

If KGO's Ward is being truthful about why he was involved with child porn, the government is treating him differently than it has former *Times*man Eichenwald. Is that because the feds don't consider Ward such a good friend as they do Eichenwald? Does the DOJ [Department of Justice] deliberately go after certain types of media people and leave others alone? It's too early to tell, since only three such individuals have been publicly implicated as involved with child porn. Meanwhile, the media has no way to cover the topic. To accurately describe the extent of the problem, to compare government claims with reality requires work that invites prosecution.

Journalists need some kind of system or First Amendment permit to allow them to do their reporting. Otherwise, the public will remain ignorant about what's really going on with child pornography. And media people trying to find out will risk indictment, or worse.

13

Journalists Do Not Need to See Child Pornography to Report on It

Alia Malek

Alia Malek is a writer based in New York City. She is a former assistant editor at the Columbia Journalism Review *and civil rights attorney in the Department of Justice.*

In a 2006 Salon *article, writer Debbie Nathan questioned how journalists could report on child pornography when it is illegal to look at such images. She referenced Kurt Eichenwald's* The New York Times *series on child pornography that contained graphic descriptions of pornographic images, asserting her assumption that the reporter had viewed these images himself. The same day that Nathan's article appeared,* Salon *pulled it and issued two corrections, one disavowing Nathan's argument that the law provides no protection for journalists covering child pornography and the other reiterating the legal disclaimer* The New York Times *had attached to Eichenwald's articles. Yet Nathan's original questions remain open for discussion. She argues that journalists must see images of child pornography for themselves rather than taking the government's word for it. But journalists who write about terrorism do not need to engage in terrorism themselves to report on it. Furthermore, there is no credible evidence that the government can not be trusted as far as determining what is child pornography. Nathan's argument also misses the point that the exploitation of children continues each time*

Alia Malek, "Child Pornography: To See, or Not to See?" *Columbia Journalism Review,* September 21, 2006. Reproduced by permission of the publisher and the author.

pornographic images are viewed. Finally, there is a real possibility that a shield intended for journalists would be used by actual pornographers to protect their criminal acts.

Writing in *Salon* on August 24 [2006], Debbie Nathan wanted to start a conversation about child pornography. She raised the question: How can journalists report on child pornography when it is a crime to even look at such images? Nathan argued that journalists should be protected from prosecution for possession of child pornography if that possession is for legitimate reporting purposes, including, for example, testing government claims about the prevalence of child pornography.

Instead, the conversation came to a screeching halt.

According to Nathan's article, her inquiry was rooted in her own research this summer into child porn on the Internet. In the course of her reporting, she inadvertently stumbled onto a Web site that featured illegal images. She became consumed with a fear that she would be arrested and prosecuted, recalling the prosecution and incarceration in 2000 of freelance journalist Lawrence Matthews in Washington, D.C. on charges that he had received and transmitted pornographic images of children in the course of his research on the topic. She reached out to other journalists and researchers who had looked into the subject, and heard stories of people abandoning the enterprise because of the risk of prosecution.

Then on August 20 [2006], *The New York Times* published a piece by Kurt Eichenwald that exposed a group of new Web sites purporting to have legal images of children but which in fact feature images that are arguably pornographic. As Eichenwald explained, courts have decided that nudity is not required for images to be deemed child pornography. The *Times* article was accompanied by a disclaimer that stated: "Covering this story raised legal issues. United States law makes it a crime to purchase, download, or view child pornography, unless the images are promptly reported to authorities and no images are copied or retained. The *Times* complied with the law, disclosing what it found to appropriate authorities."

Nathan's Argument

Eichenwald's article, beyond just reporting on the trend, included lurid descriptions of the kinds of images found on these "child modeling" sites, though he says he relied on law enforcement and chat-room descriptions of the images rather than firsthand viewing. Nathan, however, assumed that Eichenwald had seen the images himself, and kicked off her article by provocatively saying that Eichenwald had spent time recently "look[ing] at a lot of kiddie porn." Though she discussed Eichenwald's tactics and opined on their legality, she ultimately was arguing that "the government prohibits reporters and other legitimate investigators from doing front-line research into child pornography," because she believes such work requires journalists to view illegal images and risk being prosecuted.

A journalist like Nathan, who wants to see the images for her reporting, by definition would break the law and risk prosecution.

Uncontested in Nathan's argument is the notion that journalists have to actually see these images to test "government claims as to how prevalent child pornography really is and what makes an image pornographic."

On the same day Nathan's article was posted on *Salon*, the magazine pulled it and any letters it generated, and issued two corrections. The first correction emphasized that the law "does offer some legal protection for journalists and other researchers" and that an "affirmative defense may exist that would protect such work under certain circumstances, and the

opinion asserted by Nathan that her work ... would constitute a violation of the law was inaccurate."

(An affirmative defense is one that does not deny the truth
of the allegations against the defendant but gives some other
reason why the defendant cannot be held liable.)

The second correction stressed that Eichenwald's article
was "not based on reviewing the content of the sites themselves" and reiterated the legal disclaimer that the *Times* origi-
nally ran with Eichenwald's piece, asserting that journalists
who come to possess these images inadvertently and who report them to the federal authorities are protected from prosecution.

Worthy Questions

With *Salon* disavowing Nathan's entire article, the matter
seemed settled. But the two questions at the heart of this epi-
sode are worth considering. First, the question Nathan addressed in her ill-fated article: Should journalists be protected
from prosecution when they *intentionally* seek out child pornography for reporting purposes? And this one, which Eichenwald vigorously answers in the negative: Do journalists need
to see these images—and therefore break the law—to adequately report on the subject?

The *Times* limited its interpretation of the federal statute's
provision for an affirmative defense to the case of inadvertent
viewing. But a journalist like Nathan, who wants to see the
images for her reporting, by definition would break the law
and risk prosecution.

We asked [Clay] Calvert, a professor of communications
and law and codirector of the Pennsylvania Center for the
First Amendment at Pennsylvania State University, to fill us in
on the state of the law and any affirmative defenses as they
apply to journalists:

> It is still very risky for journalists today to receive and trans-
> mit, during their investigation of a story or a report, images

of child pornography. The Matthews case makes this clear in the U.S. Court of Appeals for the Fourth Circuit, and the general line of Supreme Court precedent is that journalists are not exempt from generally applicable laws that apply equally to all citizens. Clearly child pornography statutes are such laws of general applicability, so journalists take a risk today when investigating child pornography as they come across it on the Web, even with the exception spelled out in the federal statute pertaining to destruction of the images and reporting the matter to law enforcement officials. That defense under federal statute [18 U.S.C. 2252A (d)] only applies, by its terms, to the possession of "less than three images of child pornography." In other words, basically a journalist would be allowed under this defense to only possess two images, and that's not a lot of content to look at for a full-blown investigative article.

We haven't yet seen credible evidence that the press is being lied to and manipulated in this context.

Should Journalists Trust the Government?

Nathan argues that to report on child pornography, journalists will be forced to take the government's word about, for example, what these images are, where they are, who is involved, the extent of the problem, and how much revenue is generated. And by extension, so will the public. Her argument is that the government cannot be trusted.

Indeed, in May of this year [2006], a piece in *Legal Times* tried to ascertain the source of a statistic, used by Attorney General Alberto Gonzales, on the prevalence of consumers of child porn on the Internet. As it turns out, both the media and the government were using a number—that at any given time 50,000 predators are on the Internet prowling for children—that seemed to come out of thin air. The media cited the government and the government cited the media as the source for the number.

But does contesting such a government claim require viewing the images? For *Legal Times*, at least, it did not.

In a heated exchange in the comments section of the blog on Open Democracy between August 25 and September 2 [2006], Eichenwald asserted that journalists don't need to see the images to adequately report on the subject. Eichenwald quotes his own e-mail to Nathan on the blog, saying that her "apparent belief that we need to study child porn images has all the earmarks of a rubbernecking obsession on the grotesque." He argued that journalists can trust descriptions of the images given by the courts and law enforcement officials. He reiterated these comments to CJR [*Columbia Journalism Review*] Daily in a phone interview.

A Faulty Argument

This is tricky territory. We understand the importance of challenging government claims, especially when labels are used to stigmatize people and silence debate. For example, in the context of "terrorism," we have more than anecdotal evidence that the government has falsely accused individuals and misled the public. But such investigations did not require journalists to engage in terrorism themselves, or to break the law in any other way, to find out the truth.

In the context of reporting on child pornography, it seems the only reason to see the images (and thereby break the law) is to determine whether or not they are actually pornographic, and we haven't yet seen credible evidence that the press is being lied to and manipulated in this context. Some might see this as a chicken/egg problem. But the most expedient methods of accessing information are rejected by journalists all the time when those methods are illegal. Those who argue the need to see child porn to understand it too easily dismiss the fact that not only is viewing illegal, but that it also prolongs the exploitation of these children—because society has determined that merely seeing children in these poses victimizes the child. Similarly, we recognize the tension this creates with our role as the Fourth Estate.

Whether this situation necessitates a privilege analogous to what journalists seek in a federal shield law is perhaps a discussion worth having. Of course, such a discussion would require—as in the shield law debate—an examination of the question, Who is a journalist? And in a profession that requires no licensing, there is the very real danger that pedophiles could hide behind our privilege to indulge their criminality.

Organizations to Contact

The editors have compiled the following list of organizations concerned with the issues debated in this book. The descriptions are derived from materials provided by the organizations. All have publications or information available for interested readers. The list was compiled on the date of publication of the present volume; the information provided here may change. Be aware that many organizations take several weeks or longer to respond to inquiries, so allow as much time as possible.

American Civil Liberties Union (ACLU)
125 Broad Street, 18th Floor, New York, NY   10004
(888) 567-ACLU
Web site: www.aclu.org

The American Civil Liberties Union is an organization that protects First Amendment rights and rights to equal protection, due process, and privacy, through legal, legislative, and community channels. The ACLU's publications include position papers, such as *Freedom of Expression, History Repeated: The Dangers of Domestic Spying by Federal Law Enforcement*, and *The Excluded: Ideological Exclusion and the War on Ideas*, among others.

American Library Association (ALA)
50 East Huron, Chicago, IL   60611
(800) 545-2433
e-mail: ala@ala.org
Web site: www.ala.org

The American Library Association promotes and develops library services and the librarian profession to ensure access to information for all Americans. It provides professional tools to librarians and advocates on issues concerning access to information. The association's publications include the magazines *American Libraries* and *Booklist*, the quarterly journal *Information Technology and Libraries, Newsletter on Intellectual Freedom,* and numerous others.

Center for Democracy and Technology (CDT)
1634 I Street, NW, #1100, Washington, DC   20006
(202) 637-9800 • fax: (202) 637-0968
Web site: www.cdt.org

The Center for Democracy and Technology promotes democratic values and constitutional rights in the age of the Internet through research and public-policy development and advocacy. It focuses on promoting access, free expression, and democratic participation, as well as protection from government surveillance and preservation of the unique nature of the Internet. The CDT's *Policy Post* briefings include "Privacy Principles for Digital Watermarking," and its reports include *Ghosts in Our Machines: Background and Policy Proposals on the "Spyware" Problem.*

Concerned Women for America
1015 Fifteenth Street, NW, Suite 1100
Washington, DC   20005
(202) 488-7000 • fax: (202) 488-0806
Web site: www.cwfa.org

Concerned Women for America is an advocacy organization that promotes biblical values and a restoration of the American family to its traditional purpose. Its core issues are family, the sanctity of human life, education, pornography, religious liberty, and national sovereignty. It publishes the bimonthly magazine, *Family Voice.*

CyberAngels
P.O. Box 3171, Allentown, PA   18106
(610) 351-8250 • fax: (610) 482-9101
Web site: www.cyberangels.org

CyberAngels is an online safety program sponsored by the nonprofit organization Guardian Angels. It provides information and education about Internet safety to children, teens, parents, educators, and researchers. CyberAngels publishes the *CyberAngels* newsletter and the *Cyber Safety Guide*.

End Child Prostitution, Child Pornography and Trafficking of Children for Sexual Purposes (ECPAT-USA)

157 Montague Street, Brooklyn, NY 11201
(718) 935-9192 • fax: (718) 935-9173
Web site: www.ecpatusa.org

ECPAT-USA is part of the ECPAT global network of organizations working to eliminate the commercial sexual exploitation of children. The organization aims to do this through education, advocacy, and policy. ECPAT-USA publishes numerous reports including *Prostituted Youth in New York City: An Overview* and the *ECPAT Global Monitoring Report: United States of America*, as well as *ECPAT-USA News*.

First Amendment Center

Vanderbilt University, Nashville, TN 37212
(615) 727-1600 • fax: (615) 727-1319
e-mail: info@fac.org
Web site: www.firstamendmentcenter.org

The First Amendment Center is a nonpartisan center devoted to preserving and protecting First Amendment rights. The center provides education and information and serves as a forum for discussion of issues of free speech. It publishes an annual *State of the First Amendment* survey and various other publications, including *The Privacy Problem* and *Internet Filters and Public Libraries*.

Focus on the Family

8605 Explorer Drive, Colorado Springs, CO 80920
(719) 531-5181
Web site: www.family.org

Focus on the Family's mission is to spead the gospel of Jesus Christ by protecting the institution of the family and promoting biblical truths. It focuses on issues of marriage, children, the sanctity of human life, social responsibility, and gender roles. Focus on the Family publishes several magazines, including *Clubhouse, Clubhouse Jr., Brio, Citizen,* and *Plugged In,* and books, such as *False Intimacy, Focus on the Family Marriage Ministry Guide,* and *Protecting Your Child in an X-Rated World.*

The Free Expression Policy Project
170 West 76th Street, #301, New York, NY   10023
Web site: www.fepproject.org

The Free Expression Policy Project educates and advocates on issues of free speech, copyright, and media democracy. It focuses its efforts on restrictions placed on publicly funded expression and Internet content, restrictive copyright laws, mass media consolidation, and censorship aimed at children. It publishes policy reports such as *Internet Filters* and *Intellectual Property and Free Speech in the Online World,* as well as numerous white papers and fact sheets.

Free Speech Coalition
P.O. Box 10480, Canoga Park, CA   91309
(818) 348-9373 • fax: (818) 348-8893
Web site: www.freespeechcoalition.com

The Free Speech Coalition is a trade organization for the adult entertainment industry. It serves as a legislative watchdog for this industry and lobbies for increased tolerance of free sexual expression. The coalition publishes *The Free Speech X-Press* and the *State of the Industry Report.*

National Center for Missing and Exploited Children (NCMEC)
Charles B. Wang International Children's Building
Alexandria, Virginia   22314-3175
(703) 274-3900 • fax: (703) 274-2200
Web site: www.missingkids.com

The National Center for Missing and Exploited Children (NCMEC) is a nonprofit organization that works to prevent child exploitation, locate missing children, and assist victims of child abduction and exploitation. It serves as a clearing-house of information about missing and exploited children, provides assistance and training to law enforcement agencies, and provides information about legislation that promotes the protection of children. The center publishes the news bulletin *The Front Line*, the *Keeping Kids Safer on the Internet* guide, the *Online Victimization* survey, and numerous other publications.

National Coalition Against Censorship (NCAC)

275 7th Avenue, #1504, New York, NY   10001
(212) 807-6222 • fax: (212) 807-6245
e-mail: ncac@ncac.org
Web site: www.ncac.org

The National Coalition Against Censorship is an alliance of nonprofit organizations dedicated to defending freedom of thought, inquiry, and expression. The coalition educates the public about the dangers of censorship and supports organizations and activities that oppose censorship. It publishes the newsletter *NCAC Censorship News*, as well as *Censoring Culture: Contemporary Threats to Free Expression*, *Potentially Harmful: the Art of American Censorship*, and other publications.

Bibliography

Books

Yamin Akdeniz | *Internet Child Pornography and the Law.* Burlington, VT: Ashgate, 2008.

Monique Ferraro and Eoghan Casey | *Investigating Child Exploitation and Pornography: The Internet, Law, and Forensic Science.* Burlington, MA: 2004.

Chris Hansen | *To Catch a Predator: Protecting Your Kids from Online Enemies Already in Your Home.* New York: Dutton, 2007.

Stephen T. Holmes and Ronald M. Holmes | *Sex Crimes: Patterns and Behavior.* Los Angeles: Sage, 2009.

Philip Jenkins | *Beyond Tolerance: Child Pornography Online.* New York: New York University Press, 2001.

Robert Jensen | *Getting Off: Pornography and the End of Masculinity.* Cambridge, MA: South End Press, 2007.

Michael Leahy | *Porn Nation: Conquering America's #1 Addiction.* Chicago: Northfield, 2007.

Debbie Nathan | *Pornography.* Toronto, ON: Groundwood Books, 2008.

Ian O'Donnell and Claire Milner	*Child Pornography: Crimes, Computers, and Society.* Devon, UK: 2007.
Pamela Paul	*Pornified: How Pornography Is Transforming Our Lives, Our Relationships, and Our Families.* New York: Times Books, 2005.
Ethel Quayle	*Child Pornography: An Internet Crime.* New York: Routledge, 2003.
Julian Scher	*Caught in the Web: Inside the Police Hunt to Rescue Children from Online Predators.* New York: Carroll and Graf, 2007.
Frank Schmalleger and Michael Pittaro, Eds.	*Crimes of the Internet.* Upper Saddle River, NJ: Prentice Hall, 2009.

Periodicals

Ernie Allen	"In Child Pornography, Fight Harder," *Christian Science Monitor*, November 26, 2007.
James A. Baker and Melanie Krebs-Pilotti	"All Free Speech Cases Affect Journalism," *Quill*, April 2003.

| Robert Barnes | "High Court Surveys Child Pornography Law's Scope," *Washington Post*, October 31, 2007. |

| Robert Barnes | "Justices Uphold Child Porn Law; Case Involved Criminalization of 'Pandering,'" *Washington Post*, May 20, 2008. |

| Joan Biskupic | "Court Puts Child Porn Law to Test; Justices Appear Skeptical of Challengers' Arguments," *USA Today*, October 31, 2007. |

| Joan Biskupic | "Supreme Court Affirms Child Porn Law; Challengers Said Rule Could Be Used Against Legitimate Movies," *USA Today*, May 20, 2008. |

| Joshua Brockman | "Child Sex as Internet Fare, Through Eyes of a Victim," *New York Times*, April 5, 2006. |

| *Chicago Tribune* | "3 Internet Providers Agree to Block Child Porn," June 11, 2008. |

| *The Economist* | "In Praise of P2P," December 4, 2004. |

| Kurt Eichenwald | "Child Pornography Sites Face New Obstacles," *New York Times*, December 30, 2005. |

| Kurt Eichenwald | "Congress Identifies Pornography Purchasers," *New York Times*, July 14, 2006. |

Kurt Eichenwald   "Effort to Combat Child Pornography on Internet Would Close Sites," *New York Times,* September 21, 2006.

Kurt Eichenwald   "From Their Own Online World, Pedophiles Extend Their Reach," *New York Times,* August 21, 2006.

Kurt Eichenwald   "Internet Companies Divided on Plan to Fight Pornography," *New York Times,* June 28, 2006.

Brian Friel   "The War on Kiddie Porn," *National Journal,* March 25, 2006.

Robert P. George   "Private Acts, Public Interests," *First Things,* February 2006.

Linda Greenhouse   "Court Upholds Child Pornography Law, Despite Free Speech Concerns," *New York Times,* May 20, 2008.

Linda Greenhouse   "Justices Hear Arguments on Internet Pornography Law," *New York Times,* October 31, 2007.

Orrin Hatch   "Child Pornography: An Unspeakable Crime Augmented by the Court," *Notre Dame Journal of Law, Ethnics, and Public Policy* vol. 18, no. 2, 2004.

Anick Jesdanun   "Is It Censorship or Protection?; In Monitoring Online Content, Internet Companies Are Judge and Jury," *Washington Post,* July 20, 2008.

Wendy Kaminer   "Watch What You Imagine," *The Phoenix,* November 14, 2007.

Will Knight   "Chasing the Elusive Shadows of
                       e-Crime," *New Scientist*, May 8, 2004.

Wendy Koch   "Ban on Child Porn Web Forums
                       Affects Few; 'Under 1%' Use Groups
                       Blocked in ISP Deal," *USA Today*,
                       June 13, 2008.

Wendy Koch   "Parents of Child-Porn Victims Seek
                       More Funding," *USA Today*, February
                       7, 2008.

Brian Krebs   "Anti–Child-Porn Tactic Criticized;
                       Thwarting Payments Makes Users
                       Hard to Track, Report Says,"
                       Washington Post, June 11, 2008.

Adam Liptak   "If Your Hard Drive Could Testify,"
                       New York Times, January 7, 2008.

Los Angeles Times   "'Pandering' and Porn; Once Again,
                       the Supreme Court Will Rule on
                       Congress' Effort to Crack Down on
                       Child Pornography," November 10,
                       2007.

Jerry Markon   "Crackdown on Child Pornography;
                       Federal Action, Focused on Internet,
                       Sets Off a Debate," *Washington Post*,
                       December 15, 2007.

Bill McClellan   "Better to Cut Off Child Porn at the
                       Source," *St. Louis Post-Dispatch*, April
                       27, 2008.

Daniel P. Mears, Christina Mancini, Marc Gertz, Jake Bratton	"Sex Crimes, Children, and Pornography: Public Views and Public Policy," *Crime and Delinquency*, October 2008.
Neil Munro	"Regulating Fantasy," *National Journal*, June 30, 2007.
New York Times	"A Discomfiting Threat to Free Speech," May 21, 2008.
James Oliphant	"Child Porn Law Goes to High Court; Critics Say Statute Too Broad to Stand," *Chicago Tribune*, October 31, 2007.
George H. Pike	"Living in a Post-CIPA World," *Information Today*, September 2003.
David G. Savage	"Court Upholds Child-Porn Law; Messages Offering or Seeking Sexual Images of Minors—Real or Not—Will No Longer Qualify as Free Speech," *Los Angeles Times*, May 20, 2008.
Julian Scher	"The Not-So-Long Arm of the Law," *USA Today*, May 1, 2007.
Julian Scher and Benedict Carey	"Debate on Child Pornography's Link to Molesting," *New York Times*, July 19, 2007.
Ron Scherer	"To Bust Child-Porn Rings, Larger Role Sought for Internet Service Providers," *Christian Science Monitor*, February 9, 2007.

Shane Schick	"MS Helps Develop Child Porn Tracking Database," *Computing Canada*, April 22, 2005.
Regina B. Schofield	"Protecting Children in Cyberspace," *Sheriff*, September/October 2006.
John Schwartz	"Internet Filters Are: [Good] [Bad] [Both]," *New York Times*, July 4, 2004.
Alan Sears	"Grandparents and Pornographers," *Baptist Press*, April 20, 2007.
Annmarie Timmins	"File Sharing Can Spread Peril," *Concord (NH) Monitor*, March 18, 2008.
Washington Post	"Checking Child Pornography; The Supreme Court Considers a Pandering Case," October 29, 2007.
Washington Post	"Safeguarding Children; The Supreme Court Upholds a Carefully Crafted Law Targeting Child Pornographers," May 22, 2008.

Index